Before and After Baptism

The Work of Teachers and Catechists

Edited by James A. Wilde

Agnes Cunningham
Catherine Dooley
James B. Dunning
Ron Lewinski
Gilbert Ostdiek
Marie Seaman
Gerard S. Sloyan
James A. Wilde

Liturgy Training Publications

All references to the Rite of Christian Initiation of Adults (RCIA)
are based on the text and the paragraph numbers of the 1988
edition: ©1985, International Committee on English in the Liturgy;
©1988, United States Catholic Conference.

"Recovering Christian Mystagogy for Contemporary Churches"
by Ron Lewinski is based on the author's presentation at the 1988
Institute of Liturgical Studies at Valparaiso University.

"The Lectionary As a Sourcebook of Catechesis in the RCIA,"
by Catherine Dooley, first appeared in
Catechumenate: A Journal of Christian Initiation 10 (May 1988).

Liturgy Training Publications
1800 North Hermitage Avenue
Chicago IL 60622-1101
Editorial Phone: 312/486-8970
Order Phone: 312/486-7008

Printed in the United States of America

ISBN 0-930467-88-4

Design: Jane Marie Caplan
Cover design: Carolyn Riege
Cover art: from *Coptic Textile Designs* (Dover Publications)

Before and After Baptism

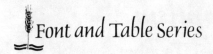

Font and Table Series

The *Font and Table Series* offers pastoral perspectives on Christian baptism, confirmation and eucharist. Other titles in the series are:

A Catechumenate Needs Everybody: Study Guides for Parish Ministers
An Easter Sourcebook: The Fifty Days
Baptism Is a Beginning
Commentaries on the Rite of Christian Initiation of Adults
Confirmation: A Parish Celebration
Finding and Forming Sponsors and Godparents
Guide for Sponsors
How Does a Person Become a Catholic?
How to Form a Catechumenate Team
Infant Baptism in the Parish: Understanding the Rite
Welcoming the New Catholic

Related and available through Liturgy Training Publications:

The Rite of Christian Initiation of Adults (Ritual Edition)
The Rite of Christian Initiation of Adults (Study Edition)

Contents

vii   Introduction

INITIATORY CATECHESIS IN THE EARLY CHURCH

1   Baptismal Catechesis in the New Testament
James A. Wilde

15   Patristic Catechesis for Baptism: A Pedagogy for Christian Living
Agnes Cunningham

CATECHESIS AND THE LECTIONARY

27   Forming Catechumens through the Lectionary
Gerard S. Sloyan

39   The Lectionary as a Sourcebook of Catechesis in the Catechumenate
Catherine Dooley

53   Prebaptismal and Postbaptismal Catechesis for Adults
James B. Dunning

CATECHESIS IN PRACTICE

67   Catechizing Families with Infants and Preschoolers
Marie Seaman

81   Recovering Christian Mystagogy for Contemporary Churches
Ron Lewinski

97   How Do Initiatory Symbols Come Alive for Adults?
Gilbert Ostdiek

Introduction

OU ARE IN GOOD COMPANY. Jesus, the apostles, Mary, Paul, Priscilla, Hippolytus, Cyril, Egeria, Chrysostom, Ambrose and many others walk with you. Like them, you demonstrate faith in the reign of God for people who want to be baptized and partake at the table of the Lord. Today, people not too different from the apostles—like Linda, Thomas, Mary Jo and Wayne—impart by word and example that same font-and-table faith.

The authors of this book look at baptismal catechesis from three different but complementary views. James Wilde and Agnes Cunningham look at history. They examine the New Testament and patristic period for the earliest understandings and practice of prebaptismal and postbaptismal catechesis. It was in these times that basic questions were framed precisely and constructively for the benefit of the whole tradition.

Gerard Sloyan, Catherine Dooley and James Dunning demonstrate the role of the lectionary in sacramental catechesis. What is a lectionary and what does it mean that this is how the church encounters the scriptures? Specifically, what is the nature of our present Roman lectionary and what place should it have in the process of initiation? The authors bring insight, imagination and challenge.

Marie Seaman, Ron Lewinski and Gilbert Ostdiek provide pastoral insight, educational theory and practical suggestions. Since infant baptism is a vital part of a parish's approach to initiation, Seaman outlines a structure that would allow a parish to care for parents, infants and young children. Lewinski discusses, in the light of the past, how mystagogy can be a moving and faith-filled experience. Ostdiek masterfully unveils the layers of initiatory symbols to show the powerful connections between them and the world of the adult catechumen and neophyte.

There are three approaches here. One shows the earliest catechetical traditions of the church. The second demonstrates how the lectionary and catechesis work together. The third brings us to the parish and home. You may seek the approach you need most, but your vision will be brightest when you let all three work together for you.

♦ *James A. Wilde*

Baptismal Catechesis in the New Testament

TO BEGIN, WE ARE INVITED to ask of the New Testament two important questions: What constituted a Christian initiatory rite and what catechesis surrounded that rite? We will ask these questions of the texts of Paul, Mark, Matthew, Luke-Acts and John. After discussing the rite of initiation, we will try to describe the *kerygma* of the major authors of the New Testament. Kerygma is the initial proclamation of gospel faith in word or action that precedes the rite of initiation, roughly corresponding to the word *evangelization* as we use it today. Then we will look at the New Testament *didache*: a "second reflection" on what happened already in the initiation rite, roughly corresponding to what came to be called *mystagogy*.

The transition in the first century from Hebrew circumcision to Christian baptism and the sources of Christian baptism have already been discussed adequately by Reginald Fuller and others.[1] The reader is strongly encouraged to study these works because this essay begins where Fuller's work ended 15 years ago with the masterful conclusion, against such influential interpreters as L. S. Thornton and H. Schlier,[2] that "the connection of the sealing with baptism is therefore unmistakable."[3] Kenan Osborne's conclusion on the same point is considerably stronger:

> The New Testament has absolutely no indication of another stage in Christian initiation which would come between baptism on the one hand and eucharist on the other. Baptism opens the door to the eucharist banquet. This lack of any intermediary situation indicates . . . first, a strong connection between baptism and eucharist, and, second, a theological anomaly to the contemporary practice of a church recognizing another Christian community's baptism but refusing eucharistic hospitality.[4]

A few things are agreed upon by all the New Testament authors, such as the centrality of Jesus' death and resurrection for our salvation, but many more things enjoy a diversity that invites explanation and makes our work interesting. When someone asks, "What is the New Testament ecclesiology?" the only honest answer is, "Well, whose do you want: Paul's, John's or Luke's?" The topic of Christian initiation in the New Testament is both unified and diverse.

Christian Initiation: One Action, Many Forms

We cannot find evidence in the New Testament favoring Christian initiation taking place through several ritual actions over extended periods of time. Rather, Christian initiation is understood throughout the New Testament as a single unitary event, a one-time experience.

Furthermore, in the New Testament, initiation is the direct result of the death and resurrection of Christ. An affirmation made by all New Testament authors is that baptism is always connected with the event of the passover of Jesus Christ. There is no evidence that by our own discipline or effort we can save ourselves. Jesus Christ alone is Savior.

Paul. The earliest author of the New Testament emphasizes several things about Christian initiation that others do not. We see some of them in Galatians 3:25—4:7, written in about 54:

> But now that faith has come, we are no longer under a disciplinarian. For

through faith you are all children of God in Christ Jesus. For all of you who were baptized into Christ have clothed yourselves with Christ. There is neither Jew nor Greek, there is neither slave nor free person, there is not male or female; for you are all one in Christ Jesus. And if you belong to Christ, then you are Abraham's descendant, heirs according to the promise.

I mean that as long as the heir is not of age, he is no different from a slave, although he is the owner of everything, but he is under the supervision of guardians and administrators until the date set by his father. In the same way we also, when we were not of age, were enslaved to the elemental powers of the world. But when the fullness of time had come, God sent his Son, born of a woman, born under the law, to ransom those under the law, so that we might receive adoption. As proof that you are children, God sent the spirit of his Son into our hearts, crying out, "Abba, Father!" So you are no longer a slave but a child, and if a child, then also an heir through God.

According to Schlier,[5] these few lines, consistent with 1 and 2 Corinthians, allude to the entire salvation history and its intimate connection with baptism. The Spirit of God, which is the Spirit of Christ, is so close to the Christian that he or she is now able to address the Holy One simply as "Abba," not through any secret epithets or complicated incantations known to the Gnostics or the practitioners of the mystery cults. In Galatians 6:15, we hear: "It does not matter if a person is circumcised or not; what matters is for him to become an altogether new creature." For Paul, the most important fact about baptism is that it gives birth to a "new creation" through adoption. Adoption as sons and daughters is a work of God in the Spirit, not our work. All we do is make an opening for God's work of adoption, and then we are new. Newness, the primary Pauline symbol for baptism, denotes new membership in the community of the Nazarene, adoption by the new God—not by one of the old, Roman deities and cult gods that were so familiar—and a completely new identity as one lovable and loved.

Forgiveness and repentance are clearly present as a baptismal theme, but beyond the idea of mere *restoration*, Paul's positive emphasis on newness and adoption is what turns slaves into sons and daughters crying "Abba," for now they enjoy the glorious freedom of the children of God.

Some of these points are made again by Paul a few years later in Romans 6:1–11, the most highly developed and coherent description of the meaning of baptism that we have in the New Testament. Note the multiple contrasts of past and present through which Paul speaks of this newness:

> What then shall we say? Shall we persist in sin that grace may abound? Of course not! How can we who have died to sin yet live in it? Or are you unaware that we who were baptized into Christ Jesus were baptized into his death? We were indeed buried with him through baptism into death, so that, just as Christ was raised from the dead by the glory of the Father, we too might live in newness of life.
>
> For if we have grown into union with him through a death like his, we shall also be united with him in the resurrection. We know that our old self was crucified with him, so that our sinful body might be done away with, that we might no longer be in slavery to sin. For a dead person has been absolved from sin. If, then, we have died with Christ, we believe that we shall also live with him. We know that Christ, raised from the dead, dies no more; death no longer has power over him. As to his death, he died to sin once and for all; as to his life, he lives for God. Consequently, you too must think of yourselves as being dead to sin and living for God in Christ Jesus.

Here Paul offers ample evidence for the mystical union between the person being baptized and the dead and risen Jesus Christ. See also Galatians 2:20, "Now I live, not I, but Christ in me." The devil, sin and death are powerless, because now Jesus and others who believe are in "risen life." Now for the Christian there is a wholly new kind of life for God in Jesus Christ: a new unifying life with Christ, with the Spirit and with the Father.

Did Paul baptize? Probably. We have no hard evidence, but circumstances point in that direction. In 1 Corinthians 6:11 Paul summarized the former life of vice that the recipients of his letter followed: "But you were washed, you were made holy, you were justified in [or "by"] the name of our Lord Jesus Christ in [or "by"] the Spirit of our God." Clearly, Paul connected the water bath with the anointing of the Spirit.

Those epistles which were probably not written by Paul, but are attributed to him, also have this note of unity with Jesus, the Spirit and Abba, Father. They develop it horizontally even more by underlining the special union among all Christians formed through baptism. The authors of Colossians and Ephesians emphasized more than Paul did that salvation is not a private matter but is worked out within a saving community.

Mark. The baptism and preaching of John, the earliest form of which is described in Mark 1:4–15, is probably the source and reason for the ministry of baptism by Jesus' followers.

> John the Baptist appeared in the desert proclaiming a baptism of repentance for the forgiveness of sins. People of the whole Judean countryside and all the inhabitants of Jerusalem were going out to him and were being baptized by him in the Jordan River as they acknowledged their sins. John was clothed in camel's hair, with a leather belt around his waist. He fed on locusts and wild honey. And this is what he proclaimed: "One mightier than I is coming after me. I am not worthy to stoop and loosen the thongs of his sandals. I have baptized you with water; he will baptize you with the holy Spirit."
>
> It happened in those days that Jesus came from Nazareth of Galilee and was baptized in the Jordan by John. On coming up out of the water he saw the heavens being torn open and the Spirit, like a dove, descending upon him. And a voice came from the heavens, "You are my beloved Son; with you I am well pleased."
>
> After John had been arrested, Jesus came to Galilee proclaiming the gospel of God: "This is the time of fulfillment. The kingdom of God is at hand. Repent, and believe in the gospel."

The best clue to the nature of Jesus' baptism is John's statement in Mark 1:8, "I have baptized you with water; he will baptize you with the Holy Spirit." Jesus' baptism is "with the Holy Spirit."

The perception of the author of the earliest gospel is that Christian initiation, as opposed to that of John, Qumran and Jewish proselyte baptism, is "with the Holy Spirit." No more information is given about the action of initiation in Mark, except that Jesus' reception of the Holy Spirit—"On coming out of the water he saw the heavens being torn open and the Spirit, like a dove, descending upon him" (Mark 1:10)—opened the door for the desert retreat and the public ministry. As soon as he was baptized, his public ministry began: "At once the Spirit drove him out into the desert" (Mark 1:12).

The similar theophany, the transfiguration (Mark 9:2–13), specifies the exact nature and conclusion of that public ministry: suffering and death. Mark connects Christian initiation with water baptism, the Holy Spirit, ministry and the cross and resurrection of Christ. Initiation itself is seen as a single action.

Matthew. The Baptizer adds a word about Jesus' baptism: "He will baptize you with the Holy Spirit *and fire*" (Matthew 3:11). Luke follows Matthew on this point (cf. Luke 3:16). Most interpreters render "fire" as synonymous with "Holy Spirit." This word both adds emphasis and reminds those who hear this gospel of what the author says about the judgment of destruction and the power believers will have from the Spirit.

The final few sentences of the Gospel of Matthew connect baptism strongly with Christian conduct and the ministry of evangelization:

> Jesus said to them, "All power in heaven and on earth has been given to me. Go, therefore, and make disciples of all nations, baptizing them in the name of the Father, and of the Son and of the holy Spirit, teaching them to observe all that I have commanded you. And behold, I am with you always, until the end of the age." (Matthew 28:18–20)

Luke–Acts. The Gospel of Luke echoes, with only a little modification, Mark and Matthew on baptism and the Holy Spirit.

In Acts 1:5, Jesus said: "John baptized with water, but in a few days you will be baptized with the Holy Spirit." Apparently, water baptism alone was considered adequate for John the Baptizer but not for Jesus' followers. Baptism with the Holy Spirit was the critical difference. Peter's speech accomplishes the same point: "Every one of you must be baptized in the name of Jesus Christ for the forgiveness of your sins, and you will receive the gift of the Holy Spirit" (Acts 2:38).

In Ephesus, Paul asked, "Did you receive the holy Spirit when you became believers?" The answer he received was, "We never even heard that there is a holy Spirit." Paul continued:

> "How were you baptized?" "With the baptism of John." Paul said, "John baptized with a baptism of repentance, telling the people to believe in the one who was to come after him, that is, in Jesus." When they heard this, they were baptized in the name of the Lord Jesus. And when Paul laid his

hands on them, the holy Spirit came upon them, and they spoke in tongues and prophesied. Altogether there were about 12 men. (Acts 19:1–7)

"Then how were you baptized?" Paul asked. A baptism of water alone was inconceivable to Paul. Receiving the bath in the name of the Lord Jesus without receiving the Holy Spirit? Impossible!

Another challenge to easy answers is the baptism of Cornelius in Acts 10:44–48:

While Peter was still speaking these things, the holy Spirit fell upon all who were listening to the word. The circumcised believers who had accompanied Peter were astounded that the gift of the holy Spirit should have been poured out on the Gentiles also, for they could hear them speaking in tongues and glorifying God. Then Peter responded, "Can anyone withhold the water for baptizing these people, who have received the holy Spirit even as we have?" He ordered them to be baptized in the name of Jesus Christ.

Things may have gotten twisted around a few times in Acts with confusion about John's baptism and a famous group of gentiles receiving the Holy Spirit before water baptism. In every case, however, Acts clearly echoes what we noted in the synoptic tradition, namely: Any time lapse between water baptism in the Lord Jesus and the sending of the gifts of the Holy Spirit is *short*. And if the delay extends longer than a few minutes or a few days, the Twelve or their representatives rush to take care of the unthinkable negligence. "Who could deprive them of water for baptism?" "Who could withhold the Holy Spirit from a believer?"

There is another aspect of baptism in Acts: Seldom does one receive baptism or the Holy Spirit alone. The hyperbole averages about 2,000. The point is made that baptism and anointing with the holy Spirit is a community ritual, not a private one.

A conclusion that we can draw is that there are no appreciable ritual sequences for initiation in Acts, except the necessary two phases of one action. Furthermore, an extended time between baptism and anointing with the Holy Spirit (or laying on of hands) is understood by the Twelve and Paul in Acts as pastoral irresponsibility.

John. Baptism is discussed often in the Fourth Gospel. In the context of the conversation between Jesus and Nicodemus (John 3:1–15), water and Spirit may mean continued emphasis on baptism and laying on of hands throughout a member's life of light and truth. This understanding of baptism is not that of a strongly evangelizing community. Rather, it serves the spiritual development of the already established community of faith.

In John 19:34, the author points to eucharist and baptism, connecting the two as the spiritual center of a Christian life of faith: "One soldier thrust his lance into his side and immediately blood and water flowed out."

Finally, on the first day of the week, the disciples rejoiced as Jesus came and stood in their midst. He breathed on them and said to them, "Receive the holy Spirit" (John 20:22). Pentecost, in John, happens on Easter. The unity of baptism, reception of the Holy Spirit and eucharist are clear in this gospel.

Catechesis before and after Baptism and Anointing

Baptism in the name of the Lord Jesus and conferral of the Holy Spirit are two sides to a single event in the New Testament. What cognitive and affective teaching preceded it and followed it?

New Testament writers write with two kinds of people in mind: nonbelievers and believers. The former receive a retelling of the main features of gospel faith in a manner that will attract them to membership. We call this kerygma. Originally in Greece, a *kerux* proclaimed the joyful message that someone important is about to arrive (often a trumpeter performed this task). Biblically, it is a proclamation of the good news that God has turned a loving face toward human beings in need. Now we call it evangelization: a reaching out with the good news of God's love and forgiveness and the invitation to love God and neighbor in return. The Rite of Christian Initiation of Adults calls the period of evangelization the *"precatechumenate."*

Believers, on the other hand, receive from New Testament writers a catechesis that is considerably different from kerygma. Because they are believers, have been baptized and have received the Spirit, they are given the *didache*: a teaching that echoes the meaning of their baptism in the Spirit and draws out its implications. In the language of Paul

Ricoeur, didache is a second reflection on the mystery that a person has experienced. Ricoeur describes it as a second naïveté, an echoing of the significance of a symbol or ritual which reaches its designated goal by touching the heart of a person in a strong, life-changing way that lasts until death. We call it "postbaptismal catechesis" or "mystagogy." It starts with the celebration of baptism in the Spirit itself and ends only at death.

Kerygma and didache are not separate parts of the New Testament writings. They are interwoven because the gospels and epistles were meant to reach both believers and nonbelievers. We look again at each of the New Testament authors we studied above, this time to get a feel for their keryma and didache.

Paul. In the letters most certainly written by Paul, his fairly consistent kerygma is:

— Jesus Christ, Lord, Savior, is now in our midst.

— He died for our sins (1 Corinthians 11:26)[6] and rose for our salvation (1 Corinthians 15:3–7).

— So believe in the Lord Jesus Christ and start conducting your life accordingly (cf. the advice found near the conclusion of all Paul's letters).

— Receive the baptism of the Holy Spirit in the Lord Jesus, for Jesus will come in judgment soon and everything will be new.

Paul's didache uses many symbols and allegories to enlighten neophytes: the body of Christ (1 Corinthians 12), the allegory of Hagar and Sarah on freedom (Galatians 4), the story of the meeting with Peter at Antioch and Jerusalem (Galatians 2). He writes letters (1 and 2 Corinthians, 1 and 2 Thessalonians) based on requests from his communities there, keeping them informed and centered. In these letters, the most prominent part is the spiritual and ethical exhortations that always appear at the end of a letter and sometimes throughout it. The Philippian letter is a notable exception. Didache in that letter takes the form of affirmation for the believers' steadfast love and courage.

Paul's moral advice sections, whether they are based on his prior knowledge of a real problem in the community of the recipients or whether they are just general, seem to reflect a cherished didache technique of Paul's. He offers lists of virtues, lists of vices, exhortations to brotherly and sisterly consideration.

What frequently determined the nature of Paul's advice was the situation in the particular community. For example, in Corinth the problem was that many considered themselves as saved by the risen Christ in a way that allowed them all kinds of "inexpediencies."[7] In Galatia, on the other hand, Judaizers were forcing believers to take on the burden of Jewish dietary prescriptions and other laws. Paul's task of didache in both cases then was to correct the error and draw the wayward back to the center of true faith: thankfulness for salvation brought by Christ in the Holy Spirit and a spiritual and ethical life that corresponded.

The lesson for us to learn from this is that Paul's kerygma and didache—like every word in the scriptures—are not stated as timeless truths. They are articulated in a context that requires our continued study and reflection.

Mark. Writing around 70, the author of the oldest gospel expected the end of the world to arrive very soon—within minutes or at least months. This imminent apocalyptic expectation was even more intense than Paul's. Therefore it became a more important dimension of the kerygma of the Gospel of Mark. In an exceptionally precarious political and war situation, Mark's kerygma looks like this:

— The end is coming very soon, but Jesus Christ will save us in the Spirit (Mark 13) on that day—

— if we become believers and take up his cross immediately (Mark 8:34) to follow him.

— As he said, "This is the time of fulfillment. The reign of God is at hand. Repent and believe in the gospel" (Mark 1:15–16).[8]

The didache of the Gospel of Mark is this: When you see Jesus forgiving people, restoring people to life, bringing people back into community with others, healing people, showing his power even over the sea and the rest of creation, exorcising people, then you know that you can do likewise if you believe and pray and also that these are small glimpses into the great magnificence of the reign of God. This reign is beginning even now and we are privileged to have learned from Jesus what it means for all of us. Soon the whole world will be transformed. Your job, meanwhile, is to proclaim this good news to the ends of the earth (Mark 13:10) so that every human being, gentile and Jew, can become a believer before it happens. There's no time to sit down and relax. Your way will be as hard as that of Jesus. Follow him in suffering, because soon all will be reversed.

Matthew. The Gospel of Matthew, written around the year 80, has a kerygma that looks like this:

— Behold, the long-desired messiah of the Jews, whom all the Hebrew Scriptures foretold, has at last arrived and is with us.

— But he is wonderfully available to Jews and gentiles alike now, therefore—

— we implore you to come to him immediately with open ears and open hearts and to obey his every command

— so that you may end up on the right side of God in heaven when the last day comes.

Matthew's apocalyptic expectation is mild compared to Mark's. Matthew begins talking about the intervening time between today and the final day; hence, he begins a strong emphasis on continued living in community (Matthew 18).

Matthew's didache is primarily an exhortation to be obedient to Jesus Christ who has radicalized the Jewish legal requirements to make them reasonable and observable. There is a call to proper conduct in the church community, an appeal to recognize Peter's authority, a strong mission to less fortunate people.

Luke–Acts. The kerygma of Luke–Acts is this:

— Jesus Christ died for us, rose from the dead for us and is now seated at the Father's right hand in heaven.

— The Holy Spirit of Jesus Christ, however, is with us powerfully and intimately during this long and difficult time of the church before the end finally comes.

— So believe in the Lord Jesus and be baptized in his name;

receive the anointing of the Spirit that makes you one of us in the community of the church.

The didache of Luke–Acts asks baptized and anointed members of the community to build a spirituality of taking up the cross of Jesus daily in helping the brothers and sisters and in following the leadership of the Holy Spirit. Invariably, it leads to the mission of evangelizing the world (Acts 1:8). The church is understood as the continual anointing of the Spirit (Acts 10),[9] an ongoing mirror of baptism in the name of Jesus and anointing with the Holy Spirit, an unending mission of evangelization.

John. Strangely, a kerygma is not highly developed in the Fourth Gospel. It seems that this gospel reflects a community whose mission is more toward fellow members than outreaching. For example, where the synoptic gospels, after the story of the miraculous catch of fish, have Jesus commanding disciples to become fishermen of people (Luke 5:1–11), John has Jesus issue the invitation, "Come for breakfast . . . and bring some fish" (John 21:12).

The didache of John is a series of signs through which members of the community of the beloved disciple[10] make deep faith decisions between light and darkness, vision and blindness, life and death, good and evil, and thus they grow in faith in the God who reveals all things through the word made flesh. The signs are actions that symbolize the cross. They are little crosses preparing the community's adherents for the great cross raised up in their life with Jesus Christ. Words such as "church," "parable," "reign of God," "last day" do not appear in John. Rather, the didache surrounds ideas such as "present judgment," "truth," "faith."

Conclusion

When we compare New Testament kerygma and didache with evangelization and mystagogy as they come to expression in the Rite of Christian Initiation of Adults, some new questions arise. Are we obfuscating some basic Christian traditions: Do we give short shrift to the biblical passages which reflect the central kerygma of God's love for us, or does our thanksgiving shine forth for all to see? Do we alibi ourselves out of God's call to membership in the community of the disciples of Christ, or do we help our brother and sister carry their cross? Do we forget being "dead to sin" in baptism, or do we immerse ourselves totally in Christ through faith, hope and love? With the Corinthians, do we say, "Now we are baptized, so we can do anything because we are risen with Christ," or do we truly recognize the body of Christ and conduct ourselves accordingly to build it up? Kerygma and didache keep us centered on the way of Jesus Christ in the church. Why look elsewhere?

♦ *James A. Wilde*

Notes

1. Reginald H. Fuller, "Christian Initiation in the New Testament," in *Made, Not Born: New Perspectives on Christian Initiation and the Catechumenate,* University of Notre Dame Liturgical Studies, The Murphy Center for Liturgical Research (Notre Dame: University of Notre Dame Press, 1976), 7–31; Kenan B. Osborne, OFM, "Holy Baptism in the New Testament," in *The Christian Sacraments of Initiation: Baptism, Confirmation, Eucharist* (New York: Paulist Press, 1987), 11–62. Note that in the section of his book devoted to confirmation, Osborne includes no chapter on its New Testament connections, as he does with baptism and eucharist.

2. L. S. Thornton, *Confirmation: Its Place in the Baptismal Mystery* (Westminster: Dacre Press, 1954); Heinrich Schlier, *Der Brief an die Galater,* Kritisch-exegetischer Kommentar über das Neue Testament 7 (Göttingen: Vandenhoeck & Ruprecht, 1971).

3. Fuller, "Christian Initiation," 25.

4. Osborne, "Holy Baptism," 60.

5. Schlier, "Galater," 97–108.

6. The social implications of "death for sin" are provocatively discussed by Wayne A. Meeks in *The First Urban Christians: The Social World of the Apostle Paul* (New Haven: Yale University Press, 1983), 150–57. Also: Eugene LaVerdiere, "The Rite of Christian Initiation of Adults: A New Testament Introduction," *Resource Book for the RCIA,* Ronald Amandolare, Thomas Ivory, William Reedy, (New York: William H. Sadlier, 1988), 118: "For Paul, even the Lord's Supper was a proclamation of the good news, indeed the ultimate proclamation" (1 Corinthians 11:26).

7. These inexpediencies are discussed by Krister Stendahl in "Justification Rather Than Forgiveness," *Paul among Jews and Gentiles* (Philadelphia: Fortress Press, 1976), 23–29.

8. Rudolf Pesch, *Naherwartungen: Tradition und Redaktion in Mk 13* (Düsseldorf: Patmos-Verlag, 1968), 242: "Dass Markus hier in verwandelter Gestalt die zentrale

Botschaft von der Nähe, wie er sie in 1:15 programmatisch geboten hat, wiedergibt, werrät die Struktur seiner Aussagen, welche auf die Botschaft von der Nähe die Anrede, die Paranese, gründen."

9. Heribert Mühlen, *Una Mystica Persona* (Göttingen: Vandenhoeck & Ruprecht, 1962), passim.

10. Raymond Brown, *The Community of the Beloved Disciple* (Philadelphia: Fortress Press, 1981), 39.

Patristic Catechesis for Baptism: A Pedagogy for Christian Living

THERE ARE RELATIVELY FEW QUESTIONS under discussion in theology today that cannot be taken to the Fathers of the church for some degree of clarification and insight. Even those issues that seem to belong specifically to our age might be addressed, perhaps, with greater courage and hope if we were more familiar with the basic teachings and principles of action of the Fathers of Christian antiquity.

On the question of baptismal catechesis, the early church Fathers are preeminent guides and mentors. They have traced a path and bequeathed a heritage for the church in every age. The restoration of the Rite of Christian Initiation of Adults and the catechumenate bears witness to the wisdom of the church in retrieving and mining the treasures of catechesis as it was understood and practiced in the patristic era.

In the following pages, I shall attempt to show the distinction between the practice of the first three centuries of the Christian era and the practice that followed in the Golden Age of the Fathers, a term commonly used to refer to the fourth and fifth centuries. I shall further distinguish between prebaptismal and postbaptismal catechesis in each of those time periods. I shall also investigate the manner in which catechetical instruction in early Christianity was influenced by liturgical, doctrinal and pastoral factors. In a few concluding reflections I shall attempt to indicate how we can understand patristic catechesis as a pedagogy for Christian living.

The Ante-Nicene Period (95–325)

The *Apostolic Tradition*, ordinarily attributed to Hippolytus of Rome, is generally recognized as the one document that provides information about the catechumenate for the period prior to the Council of Nicaea.[1] Another source from this same age is the most ancient extant treatise on baptism, *De baptismo*, written by Tertullian. In addition, the homilies of Origen and certain texts found in early documents explaining the Christian life help us to arrive at some notion of pre-Nicene catechesis, despite the absence of an abundance of material from that era. Because of the lack of historical data, it is difficult to reconstruct in detail either prebaptismal or postbaptismal catechetical practice in the first three centuries.

Prebaptismal Catechesis. Despite the absence of documents witnessing to the details of structure and content of the catechumenate before Nicaea, it is possible to find evidence of the elements of liturgy, doctrine and pastoral concern in the catechesis of that period. *Liturgically*, catechumens were introduced to the observance of the Lord's Day, a practice solemnized from apostolic times.[2] Closely related to this observance was the celebration of the resurrection, a feast kept by Christians everywhere, although not always on Sunday.[3]

An important dimension of the liturgical aspect of the early catechumenate was the role of the community in the preparation of the candidate. The day of the Lord became the occasion par excellence for the gathering of the community. This was because there were, as the *Didache* affirms, prophets and doctors, as there had been apostles and as there were to be bishops and deacons, to assure the celebration of the eucharist.[4] Catechesis, as Hippolytus and Origen testify, took place within these celebrations.[5] Catechumens were introduced to Christian prayer through a praying community. They were led toward membership in an *ekklesia*, assembled in *koinonia* as a community of faith, love and worship, in expectation of the coming of the kingdom in its fullness.

In addition to the liturgical element, catechesis in the early Christian centuries included instruction in preparation for Christian initiation. What was the nature of this instruction? How can we describe the *doctrinal* content of the catechumenate? The answer to these questions is twofold. On the one hand, readings constituted an essential part of the Sunday liturgy, as of every liturgical gathering. Selections from the gospel accounts, the psalms, the letters of Paul and other writers were chosen for the benefit of the entire community, which included catechumens for that part of the celebration. The readings became even more significant instructionally, as baptism was definitively incorporated into the resurrection celebration. The story of the exodus, the images of water, the sacrificial lamb and the cross all spoke eloquently to the neophytes, reminding them of what they had heard during the time of their preparation.[6]

On the other hand, *doctrine* was imparted to the catechumen through instruction based on the rule of faith (*regula fidei*). Irenaeus explains this rule in three articles: God the Father, creator of the universe; the Word and Son of God, Jesus Christ our Lord; the Holy Spirit. Those who are baptized, according to Irenaeus, receive the Spirit of God who presents them to the Word, that is, to the Son. The Son accepts them and offers them to the Father.[7] Tertullian also affirms a rule of faith, explaining in *De baptismo* (6, 2) that the confession of faith as well as the promise of salvation are guaranteed by the three, symbolized in the triple immersion.

Pastoral concern regarding candidates in the first three centuries was expressed in texts that highlight the character of the life-style expected of a Christian. A period of initial interest and inquiry, the precatechumenate, gave an individual the opportunity to turn from the worship of familiar idols and demonstrate the desire to live a virtuous life.[8] Tertullian speaks of repentance and sincerity;[9] Justin seeks candidates who can show their willingness to pursue a life befitting a Christian.[10]

The catechumens followed a strict discipline of prayer and fasting during the prebaptismal program. They were being prepared to be "soldiers of Christ." Martyrdom was a possibility also during the first three centuries. The delayed introduction of forgiving sins committed after baptism or the initial accommodation of a single forgiveness emphasized the integrity of faith and holiness to which a Christian was called. One who was to be baptized into the death and resurrection of Christ stood before two "ways": the way of darkness and death, the way of light and life.[11]

Postbaptismal Catechesis. The existence of a formal postbaptismal cate-chesis prior to the fourth century cannot be determined with any degree of certitude. Persecutions and the uncertain situation of Chris-tianity in Roman society in general militated against a structured institution of that kind. Rather, the elements of liturgical celebration, doctrinal instruction and pastoral concern found in the preparations for Christian initiation were continued and intensified through full mem-bership in the community.

Baptism was the entrance into full participation in the entire celebration of the eucharist. Baptism was that "revolutionary" experi-ence that imparted light and strength to pursue a life of prayer and fasting in company with a praying community that had been "exor-cised" and "enlightened." Baptism was initiation to a life that would be sustained and challenged through prolonged instruction, admonition and exhortation in the preaching that was, essentially, a response to the Lord's mandate to proclaim the gospel to all people even to the end of this world.[12]

Along with the assured presence and guidance of a believing community, the neophyte frequently experienced the support and comfort of a spiritual companion or mentor. The "sponsor," who had carried responsibility for giving testimony to the initial desire of one who had discovered the good news, shared also in the program of evangelization and preparation for baptism. Postbaptismal "spiritual companioning" was not an uncommon practice. In some instances it was one of the ministries entrusted to the deacon who had assisted the bishop in the instruction of the catechumens.

Despite the lack of documentation regarding the structure and content of the catechumenate in the first three centuries of the Chris-tian era, there is sufficient evidence for us to reject the mistaken notion that formal preparation for baptism was an exclusively fourth-century phenomenon. The rites of Christian initiation were an essential dimension of the apostolic tradition, adapted to the needs and challenges of each succeeding generation in the patristic age.

The Golden Age of the Fathers (325–431)

The significance of the Golden Age of the Fathers is beyond question. From this era the church continues to receive, even today, a rich heritage of theological and spiritual doctrine. In many areas the achievements of the great Fathers of the fourth and fifth centuries have never been surpassed. In the legacy of this period is a treasury of catechetical instructions and homilies, attesting to the structure and content of a highly organized program of preparation for Christian initiation. The elements of liturgical celebration, doctrinal teaching and pastoral concern can still be found in the material to which we have access. The focus and nature of these elements, however, differ in many ways from their earlier forms. The documents tell us clearly that the church has reached a new stage in her growth and development.

Prebaptismal Catechesis. By the beginning of the fourth century, the catechumenate included four distinct stages. The first and longest period was intended for those who expressed an interest in the Christian way of life. Prospective candidates for baptism, who then became known as "catechumens" properly so-called (*accedentes*), were admitted to a second stage. A third stage was reserved for those whose petition for baptism had been approved. The fourth and final stage consisted of postbaptismal catechesis.

Ordinarily six "steps" belonged in the third period. Since the rites of initiation were normally celebrated at Easter, the season of Lent was the time for candidates to enter this stage of immediate preparation for baptism. Following the "petition" to enlist and the acceptance by the bishop, candidates were ready for the scrutiny and exorcism (1) to assure the worthiness for baptism. Those admitted to this ceremony were known as "applicants" (*competentes*), the "chosen" (*electi*) or "those to be enlightened" (*illuminandi*). They were expected to assist faithfully at the meetings (2) presided over by the bishop. Instructions (3) given by the bishop or, in some instances, by a deacon appointed by him[13] and the practice of penance (4) in witness to the desire to live a Christian life were essential to this stage. So also was the confession of one's sins (5) and a prebaptismal bath (6).[14]

The liturgical element of this prebaptismal stage was assured in several ways. Instructions took place within the season of Lent. They were given daily, or with a day's interval as each set of instructions was completed. In Jerusalem, according to one account, meetings were held only on days of fasting, that is, daily, except for Saturday and Sunday.[15] The presence and presidency of the bishop or his official representative added another liturgical dimension. So did the assembled community of candidates, "sponsors" or godparents and any of the baptized who might choose to attend. The custom of separating women and men in liturgical celebrations was followed in these catechetical gatherings.

As far as the doctrinal element was concerned, the prebaptismal instructions in the fourth and fifth centuries were based on the Lord's Prayer and the creed. The 24 catechetical lectures of St. Cyril of Jerusalem, as the most representative collection of a set of instructions available to us, included: four lectures on "one God, the Father Almighty, Creator," two lectures on the Holy Spirit, one on the resurrection and ascension, one on the church and one on the resurrection of the flesh and life everlasting.

The articles of the creed and the Lord's Prayer were "handed over" one by one. The entrusting of the creed to the candidates (*Traditio Symboli*) was a solemn and sacred act. The words had to be learned by heart to be given back (*Redditio Symboli*) in a ceremony prior to baptism.[16] Godparents were responsible for helping the candidates learn and understand the lessons in which they had been instructed.

Prebaptismal instructions were characterized by frequent quotations from scripture. As doctrine was imparted to the candidates, so was the content of the sacred writings and of the oral *traditio*, the apostolic tradition. The explanations given in the instructions were meant to provide a knowledge of Christian teachings and the motivation to strive for a life of Christian moral fidelity.

The element of pastoral concern in this era is reflected in unique and, at times, unexpected ways. In his First Catechetical Instruction, St. Augustine exhorts the deacon, Deogratias, to attend to the diversity represented in the candidates (*accedentes*) who listen to him:

It likewise makes a great difference . . . whether there are few or many; whether learned or unlearned, or a mixed audience made up of both classes; whether they are townsfolk or countryfolk, or both together; or a gathering in which all sorts and conditions of men [*sic*] are represented.[17]

In the Procatechesis, the prologue to the catechetical lectures, Cyril of Jerusalem exhorts his "dear candidates for enlightenment" to reflect on "the desire of heavenly citizenship," the "holy resolve," the "sincerity of resolution" that have led them to be "called." He explores the motives that bring his hearers to the assembly. He accepts the least reason, no matter how "unworthy" it may seem:

Maybe you did not know where you were going or what sort of net it was in which you were to be caught. You are a fish caught in the net of the church. Let yourself be taken alive; don't try to escape.[18]

St. John Chrysostom develops the theme of beauty with which baptism will enhance the candidates who are called as brides or grooms in a "spiritual marriage."[19] Like other Fathers, Chrysostom emphasizes two points in his concern for the candidates: the importance of their fidelity in attending the instructions, studying the lessons and taking them to heart; the necessity of keeping before the "eyes of their heart" the ideal to which they have been "called," the holiness for which they have been "chosen." Such exhortations were not to end with the rites of Christian initiation.

Postbaptismal Catechesis. Postbaptismal catechesis in the Golden Age of the Fathers has been summed up in one word: *mystagogy.* What is the meaning of this term, and what does it tell us about the fourth stage of the catechumenate, reserved to the neophytes, the newly baptized?

If we search the ancient documents for a definition of mystagogy, we find several suggestions that, like so many beams of light, point out to us the path along which we must go. Mystagogy is equated with Easter, with the mysteries, with the sacraments. What can we learn from even these three terms?

The mystagogical lectures were delivered during Easter week. In other words, they followed the entrance of the candidates into the church through the rites of initiation: baptism, confirmation, eucharist. The overwhelming, "awe-inspiring" rites that took place during the night of the celebration of Christ's death and resurrection had brought the candidates through the waters of creation and the exodus. They emerged from darkness to light; from death to life: in Christ, with his bride, the church, mother of those born of water and the fire of the Spirit.

The mystagogical lectures were explanations of the *mysteries* hidden from those who had, first of all, to be "enlightened" to see "spiritual, heavenly" realities with eyes of faith. Cyril of Jerusalem introduces the neophytes to his understanding of these postbaptismal instructions:

> On the principle that seeing is believing, I delayed until the present occasion, calculating that after what you saw on that night I should find you a readier audience now when I am to be your guide to the brighter and more fragrant meadows of this second Eden.[20]

St. Ambrose speaks in a similar way to the newly baptized in his church:

> If we had thought that this should have been taught those not yet initiated before baptism, we would be considered to have betrayed rather than to have portrayed the mysteries. So open your ears and enjoy the good odor of eternal life which has been breathed upon you.[21]

Theodore of Mopsuestia presents another understanding of the mysteries:

> In this way, by putting our lives in order, by recognizing the greatness of the mysteries, that invaluable gift to which we had been invited and which will put us in debt all our lives long, and by taking due care to correct our faults, we shall show ourselves worthy of our future hope.[22]

The mystagogical lectures were a preparation for sacramental living. It was only because the newly baptized had experienced the sacraments of baptism, confirmation and eucharist that they could be prepared to live a life of faithfulness to Christ, risen Lord and savior. In the postbaptismal instructions, doctrine was transmitted through reflection on each moment of the initiation rites. The liturgical celebration of the sacraments became a bridge to the Christ–Event, prefigured in the Old Testament, as well as to that eschatological moment when he would return in glory. The purpose of the mystagogical lectures expressed the pastoral concern that Christians be prepared for the ultimate day of the Lord:

Let your sanctity, informed by sacerdotal instructions, labor to maintain what it has received, that your prayer may be acceptable to God, and your oblation be as a pure victim, and that he may always recognize his sign in you, that you yourselves also may be able to come to the grace and the rewards of virtues, through our Lord Jesus Christ, to whom is honor and glory, praise, perpetuity from the ages and now and always, and for ever and ever. Amen.[23]

Concluding Reflections

As Jourjon has pointed out,[24] mystagogy is based on a number of principles, one of which is preeminently pastoral. This principle can be expressed in the following words: Only that which has been experientially lived can be the subject of a spiritual discourse. Catechesis is meant to lead a catechumen to the experience of the Christian life by a life that is Christian even before initiation through the sacramental rites. The Christian life implies a moral code, a life of prayer and a journey in faith that can be pursued only because of instructions given after the sacraments have been initially experienced.

What is the lesson in this for us? I would like to suggest that we can learn from the catechesis that comes to us from the Fathers of the church a pedagogy for Christian living. To some extent, the Rite of Christian Initiation of Adults has begun to explore ways in which this can be done. Our learning from the tradition of patristic catechesis, however, has been incomplete. As St. Ambrose would tell us, we need a threefold program: a catechesis of evangelization, to bring the gospel to non-Christians; a catechesis for sacramental living, through the full range of the catechumenate; a catechesis of the mystery of the cross, whereby we learn from the death of the Lord how to live the mystery of his resurrection.[25]

Another lesson to be learned more fully from the early Fathers is the manner in which liturgical, doctrinal and pastoral elements were integrated into the full range of baptismal catechesis, from evangelization to mystagogy. Preparation for the rites of Christian initiation, both prebaptismal and postbaptismal, throughout the entire patristic era still holds riches for us to investigate. The concept of a pedagogy for Christian living inspired by the catechesis of the Fathers of the early church is one that offers challenge and support to the church today, as she seeks to follow the mandate of her Lord:

> Go, therefore, and make disciples of all the nations. Baptize them in the name of the Father, and of the Son, and of the Holy Spirit. Teach them to carry out everything I have commanded you. (Matthew 28:19-20)

The practice of baptismal catechesis in the patristic age needs to be explored, reflected on and mined more fully than it has been until now.

♦ *Agnes Cunningham,* SSCM

Notes

1. Cf. Michel Dujarier, *The Rites of Christian Initiation* (New York: William H. Sadlier, Inc., 1979), 35; Maurice Jourjon, *Les Sacrements de la Liberté Chrétienne* (Paris: Les Edition du Cerf, 1981), 40–41; Edward Yarnold, SJ, *The Awe-Inspiring Rites of Initiation* (Great Britain: St. Paul Publications, 1972), 265–70.

2. Cf. A. Hamman, OFM, ed., *The Paschal Mystery* (New York: Alba House, 1969), 10–11.

3. The Quartodeciman question surfaced in the times of Pope Sixtus (c. 120), Pope Anicetus (c. 155) and Pope Victor (c. 178). It was settled at the Council of Nicaea in favor of the Roman practice still followed today.

4. Cf. Jourjon, *Sacrements*, 101–03.

5. Cf. *Apostolic Tradition*, 18–19; *Homélies sur Jérémie*, Source Chrétiennes 1, 105–12.

6. Hippolytus indicates that the catechumenate was to last at least three years. Yarnold (*Rites*, 7) points out that the program actually was often longer until the church understood that sins committed after baptism could be forgiven.

7. Cf. *Demonstration of the Apostolic Preaching*, 6–7; also, Dujarier, Jourjon, Yarnold for discussions of this text and those referred to in notes 8, 9, 10 and 11.

8. Cf. *Against Celsus* 3, 51, 2.

9. Cf. *On Penance* 6.

10. Cf. *Apology* 1, 61.2.

11. Cf. *Didaché* and the *Letter to Barnabas.*

12. Cf. Matthew 28:19.

13. St. Augustine's *First Catechetical Instruction* was written for a deacon friend of his at Carthage who sought guidance for a more effective method of catechizing.

14. The purpose of this bath seems to have been hygienic.

15. This is the testimony given by Aetheria (Egeria) in her diary.

16. The practice of transmitting the truths of the Christian faith orally was related to the *Disciplina Arcani* (Discipline of the Secret), by which the teachings of the church were safeguarded from pagans of candidates who did not persevere to baptism.

17. 15 (23).

18. (5).

19. "The First Instruction," 3.

20. "First Lecture on the Mysteries" (1).

21. "On the Mysteries" 1, (2)–(3).

22. Quoted in Yarnold, *Rites,* 263.

23. "On the Sacraments" 5, (126).

24. Jourjon, *Sacraments,* 119–26.

25. Ambrose, Sacraments, 111–12.

BIBLIOGRAPHY OF PATRISTIC SOURCES

Ambrose of Milan, *The Mysteries: The Sacraments* (R. J. Deferrari, translator), Fathers of the Church 44 (Washington DC: The Catholic University of America Press, 1963).

Augustine of Hippo, *The First Catechetical Instruction* (J. P. Christopher, translator), Ancient Christian Writers 2 (Westminster MD: The Newman Publishing Co., 1946).

Cyril of Jerusalem, *Procatechesis and Catecheses* 1–2 (McCauley and Stephenson, translators), Fathers of the Church 61 (Washington DC: The Catholic University of America Press, 1963).

———— , *The Works of Saint Cyril of Jerusalem* 2 (McCauley and Stephenson, translators), Fathers of the Church 64 (Washington DC: The Catholic University of America Press, 1970).

John Chrysostom, *Baptismal Instructions* (P. W. Harkins, translator), Ancient Christian Writers 31 (Westminster MD: The Newman Press, 1963).

Rufinus, *A Commentary on the Apostles' Creed* (J. N. D. Kelly, translator), Ancient Christian Writers 20 (Westminster MD: The Newman Press, 1955).

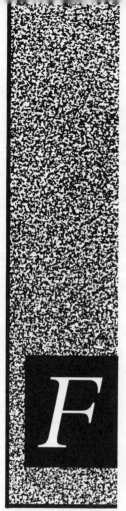

Forming Catechumens through the Lectionary

F IFTY YEARS AGO I entered a strange new world called a "major seminary," a six-year academic course, and learned that we could not begin to eat the midday or evening meal on that planet until we had listened to a lengthy account of the conquest of Canaan from the book of Joshua. After that, the silverware and dishes began to clatter but not before a modern book of piety had begun to be read, and so throughout the meal. Much later I learned that a portion of public reading, which followed a bookmark making its way through the Bible, was called a "collation." This term described a practice that made its way into religious houses of every sort and came to describe the amount of food one consumed during such a reading. Some methodical people still read a portion of scripture that way every day. A few read a chapter of the Bible daily on good days and bad. Many, including not a few Catholics, never read the Bible at all.

Continuous Reading of the Bible

The continuous-reading technique seems to have been employed in public assemblies such as the eucharistic liturgy and the divine office (or daily prayer) from very early times. It survives in the form of the first reading from the Bible at weekday Mass and the second reading on Sundays. There it is described as "semicontinuous" because the parts considered less germane to the needs of a modern congregation are omitted. The weekday selections go in the order in which the books occur in Christian Bibles. On Sundays the second reading from the epistles of St. Paul and the other apostolic writers generally occur in the same sequence. But occasionally the order is not the same as that which marked the earliest codices and is still employed in printed Bibles.

While the practice of reading a portion of the Bible before a meal is monastic, the reading of more than one portion at a liturgical assembly goes back to the early second century, perhaps earlier. If the technique of continuous readings is not used, a list of specified readings is called a lectionary. It is the earliest way Christians—many of whom, for centuries, could not read—became familiar with the Bible. Lectionary readings are the way those Christians who prepare catechumens for baptism and the newly baptized are most likely to proclaim and hear the Bible. Reading the scriptures privately and studying them in groups are excellent ideas. The ancient way is the one guaranteed to go on uninterrupted for a lifetime.

If this kind of exposure to God's word characterizes people who are candidates for baptism (or entrance into the Catholic communion), its purpose should be examined carefully so that it can achieve the maximum effect. Understanding what you hear is important. Knowing what to listen for is half the secret. Candidates for baptism or reception into the church have already experienced the mysterious lure of a faith tradition they only dimly comprehended. They feel themselves drawn to membership in a certain religious company. They have the conviction that God is somehow in its midst. The person of Jesus under his title "the Christ" exerts a strong attraction on them. Who is he and how can they know more of him, catechumens wonder. He is a person of mystery whom the four gospels partially disclose as the earthly Jesus, and they and the rest of the New Testament books as the glorified Christ. Taken together, the gospels conceal as much as they reveal. Still, the candidate for new life in Jesus cannot get enough of the evangelists' four distinct proclamations of this person.

The lectionary now in use for almost two decades provides for this need by reading from Matthew's gospel on the Sundays of one year, then Mark's, then Luke's. Great feasts of Christ and those of Mary and the apostles sometimes replace the Sunday in the calendar, thereby breaking the flow. Readings from the gospel according to John are inserted and hence do the same in all three years. In Advent and Lent the overall scheme is replaced by another. There is, however, a predominance of attention to Jesus in any given year as Matthew or Mark or Luke sees him. That means that some reading and study about a particular synoptic evangelist as these three are called (their parallel similarities and differences being able to be taken in "with one glance") is in order each year. Attention to how John resembles—and differs from—the other three is fitting in any year.

A major problem is that readings from the gospels over the three-year cycle can leave the impression on even the most diligent hearer that the purpose of the lectionary is to get all the incidents of Jesus' life read at least once during the period. And, indeed, that is the principle on which the lectionary was framed. The technique is ancient. It is described as a "gospel harmony," meaning harmonization. The first person to compose one was named Tatian, who did it, probably in Syriac, sometime around 175. He used John's gospel as his framework because of its three-Passover scheme and inserted into it incidents from the other three gospels. A modern lectionary composed on a principle more faithful to the artistry and intention of each evangelist would be distributed over four years, not three. It would not be interrupted by selections from other gospels on feasts or during seasons. And it would provide substantially longer readings. That plan might help worshipers come away at the end of a liturgical year with a genuine appreciation of the evangelist whose work they had been following. It would also encourage homilists to preach on Mark's proclamation of Jesus Christ or John's or whoever it might be. At present this is not easy to do, even in the Mark year, and certainly not as regards John.

The best, however, is the enemy of the good, as the French proverb says. Also, a plea for the immediate rearrangement of the liturgical universe may fall on deaf ears. Lectionaries were devised before anyone dreamed that Matthew's proclamation was notably different in intention from Mark's or that he did not have in mind the simple desire to present more material than the shorter (but wordier) Mark. Until this century, in fact, Mark was thought to have been the abbreviation of Matthew.

Wisdom lies in considering the Roman lectionary that *is*. How can it aid in the Christian formation of catechumens now and help them hear the Bible fruitfully in the assembly for the rest of their lives?

The first step is directing them to listen carefully for the way any given gospel passage proclaims Jesus as God's choice to achieve Israel's redemption and then the world's. Keeping one's ears alert for that is the key to all. Each time the Christian community assembles to give God thanks and praise, that is the only item on its agenda. Who is this Jesus that faith in his death and resurrection can make all the difference? Why should eating his body and drinking his blood make available to those who do it in faith the very righteousness of God? Every word that he utters, every sign of God's impending rule that he works, every promise of beatitude or threat of reprobation he expresses is an aspect of the one mystery of God we call human redemption. Candidates enrolled in the rite of initiation need help above all in listening for the redemptive word proclaimed at the heart of every passage of the gospel.

The gospels in their entirety are a word of life. Any portion, however isolated from its place in a gospel where it has maximum significance, will make sense in the ears of believers once they identify it as a redemptive word. This is not always easy to do. A parable has many details that can distract. Does the "kingdom of heaven" mean "going to heaven" as it seems? Most often it does not. And how can the gentle Jesus issue such harsh threats as he does, especially in Matthew and John? What is going on in the lectionary's gospel selection of which the hearer can be sure, whether there is a helpful homily delivered or not? Neophytes need real help in what to listen for in the gospel. They also have a couple of years in which to do so, putting their questions to the instructional team. Later, as the baptized, this marvelous opportunity may pass. Both teachers and learners should take full advantage of it. Both need to discern how the reign or rule of God is being proclaimed in every gospel passage that is read.

The Gospels and the First Readings

The gospel selections govern the choices of the first reading from the Hebrew Bible. That is the second principle of lectionary construction every Christian should know (the first one being that of the Matthew, Mark and Luke years with John interspersed). How does the gospel reading "govern" the choices from the Hebrew Scriptures? In two ways, one general and one particular. In a general way, the love story between God and Israel is the context of the "God so loved the world" story in which one Jew, Jesus, is the central figure. In particular, a biblical passage is chosen because some feature of it—its whole drift, a sentence or two or even a word—triggers the mind to prepare for the gospel reading. The technique is called typology. Stories, persons or phrases are thought to be "types" of Christ, i.e., foreshadowings in figure. He and what happened to him in a gospel passage is the "antitype," i.e., a corresponding figure. It is not an easy exercise for us to engage in. The people of Bible times, however, up to the time Jewish and Christian lectionaries were formulated were familiar with this matching game. It made great sense to them. It may make sense to us, but it is more likely that it will not. New Christians or new Catholics need help in understanding what is going on here. They may know the Bible well from their upbringing and never have been introduced to the notion of typology, or they may not know any of the first testament readings at all. How can they hear them most profitably?

Being launched on a Bible-reading career from the time they first enroll is the best way. But not everyone who is drawn to God is a reader, and some who can read do not read much at all. Meanwhile, all who are called to faith are hearers whether they have the gift of hearing or not. They can be given help and alerted to follow the first reading in a way that makes a mental note of its main thrust. What is the passage saying? Is Moses or some other prophet acting as Israel's teacher in it—praiser, admonisher, scolder? What is this patriarch or king up to in what is being read? Is it just a piece of ethical counsel, easy to understand? Sometimes the teaching is simply of the latter kind: how to act well under the terms of the covenant. At other times the whole sweep of this people's history is in question. The modern worshiper wonders who the people are with those strange Babylonian and Hebrew names. In all such cases of narrative history the thing to look for is the point the story illustrates, for the gospel reading is bound to be something closely paralleled in Jesus' career. The reason is simple. The evangelist wrote up Jesus' career with a careful backward look at Israel's history.

It is not easy to master the typological relation between the first reading—normally but not always from the Hebrew Scriptures—and the gospel reading. Many Catholics spend a lifetime missing it except when there is a very close parallel. Here, modern catechumens have a distinct advantage over "cradle Catholics." Instructors who have a taste for the Bible and a moderate amount of learning can point out this relation to them on a weekly basis.

Nothing during the period of formation precedes in importance attention to the Bible as it is shared at the weekly assembly. A congregation may be blessed with good homilies or poor, perhaps a mixture of the two, but an RCIA team can count on them only as supplementary to its task. This is a time for the methodical exploration of the Bible in the form in which it will reach the ears of believers for a lifetime. Whatever else is shared about life in Christ (in this case Catholic life), be it ethical or doctrinal or disciplinary, the biblical message is its bedrock. All other teaching is built on the word of God.

When the scriptures are shared in this optimum prebaptismal setting neither the ones doing the forming nor those being formed should set the agenda. The lectionary choices are a human work but they always let the Bible be the Bible. People have life problems, to be sure. Everyone does. But the scriptures are not a book of oracles designed to tell people when to invest and how much, or whom to marry, or how to deal with a son-in-law who does not view his wife as the treasure her doting mother does. These scriptures speak to the life situations of millions in the most varied human contexts. They do it, however, through telling about a people that has been called to serve God as a people.

The Bible is a community book. It tells about a life oriented primarily to peoplehood, not to individual experience of God. The life of the people of Israel is its earliest concern, then the natural flowering of that people which is the larger community of faith drawn from all the peoples of the earth. If every first and third reading is viewed under that aspect, it will consistently yield meaning. Should Bible study become a series of searches into "what this passage means for me," some trivial meanings will emerge and the Bible's meaning be lost.

Relation to a people is its basic meaning: the people Israel and the people church, which are one and not two in the Christian view. Any other message the Bible seems to yield will be falsely derived if this is not seen. Because such is scripture's meaning to its authors, divine and human, the profit to individuals will be immense once they grasp it. All the unfamiliar references to Israel's pagan neighbors and the puzzling aspects of Jesus' speech and behavior, even in the company of his friends, will come clear, once the main thread is identified. This is the story of God's address to a people to fulfill a loving design for it. When that is seen, the puzzling details have a chance of falling into place.

Take, for example, the gospel passage on Epiphany. It is Matthew 2:1–12 and will be familiar to many enrolled in the catechumenate as the story of the visit of the wise men from the East. Why does Matthew tell this tale of pagan stargazers whom he calls *magoi*? It is part of his contrast between a despotic king who is faithless to Israel's hopes and some learned non-Jews who practice astrology yet believe in Israel's newborn king. The transition of belief in Jesus from the first Jewish hearers to a church that would have many non-Jews as well is at the heart of Matthew's gospel. The theme begins with the gentile women Rahab and Ruth (and Bathsheba, a Hittite like her husband?) in Jesus' genealogy. It proceeds immediately to this story of Bethlehem's importance—which Matthew reverses from a snatch in the book of Micah about its unimportance! He is doing no less than giving a biblical reason why the infant child is the long-expected King-Messiah. What reason from the Bible? The first reading provides the clue. The 60th chapter of Isaiah is part of a long poem that tells about pagans in darkness and Jews basking in the light of their Lord. In the first six verses which are the reading for Epiphany, "nations" and "kings"—key words to describe non-Jews—will walk by Israel's radiance. Camel caravans will come up from the desert to place the wealth of nations—frankincense and gold—before Israel's king, the LORD, whom this tiny, despised people represents. It is Middle Eastern history stood on its head by the prophet-poet. Matthew then tells a tale that proclaims jubilantly: "It all happened! It all came true! 'I will enhance the splendor of my house' (Isaiah 60:7), the house over which the star came to a standstill" (Matthew 2:11).

You can play that game with any first and third reading, even though at times the correspondences will not be so close. What is important is not the details but the whole narrative of both testaments, of which any two such readings are a part. For the evangelists the life of

Jesus was interchangeable with the life of Israel. Believers to whom both are proclaimed see their lives as part of the same story. But this can happen only if they know the story itself in its earlier and later parts. Christians are a people of the Bible as it continues to be lived over the ages. For that to be true they must know the script. Otherwise they can have no meaningful part in the play.

Second Readings in the Liturgy

We have not until now had much to say about the second readings. They are taken from the nongospel books of the New Testament, therefore, chiefly the epistolary writings. They tend to be hortatory, the technical term for which is "paraenetic." That puts them solidly in the catechumenal tradition of the early church which employed the Bible for ethical formation before any of the Christian mysteries were shared.

Most of the second readings feature the conduct that befits the baptized. They tend to be from Paul at his warmhearted best or some anonymous writer whose letter has long been attributed to an apostolic figure. It is not of much use to trace a pattern in these second readings because the major feasts and the seasons of Lent and Advent place all three readings in a thematic relation. In doing so they interrupt any sequence. Even at that, the most you get are six or eight successive Sunday readings from one long epistle of Paul. Even that is a fairly infrequent occurrence in the three-year cycle.

The important interruption comes from another source, however, namely Paul himself breaking in on Paul. This occurs when some of his marvelous, practical advice, suitable for any age of church life, alternates with a terribly time- or place-conditioned passage that creates more problems for moderns than it solves. The apostle on gender roles (for example, in 1 Corinthians 11) in the ancient Jewish world needs a full-scale exposition not just the rapid reading of six verses which assumes a familiarity with it. The same is true of some of his most complex ideas proposed for public reading, for example the Sarah-Hagar "allegory," as he calls it (see Galatians 4). That selection is the very opposite of helpful to modern Christians who need to place modern Jews and Judaism in perspective. It is not that the great Pauline developments have no place on the Christian lectern, but that the length of the second reading never permits them sufficient opportunity to be followed intelligently. These passages end by making the hearer not know what to expect when the name of Paul or the title "Revelation" or "to the Hebrews" is announced.

The transition from one Sunday to the next may be one in St. Paul anywhere from his pastoral best to his eschatological (fine for *his* hearers; he had soaked them in it!) worst. The net effect can be dizzying. Modern mental circuits are in danger of overload, not simply because of the three readings each Sunday, but because, to convey a particularly memorable phrase in a Pauline letter, a very dense context necessarily accompanies it.

What, then, to do if the lectionary is to be employed as an effective moral formative device for prospective entrants into the church? A decision must first be made as to how much of a Sunday morning's or an evening's session is to be devoted to this exposition: a brief time always or a long time on certain occasions? The next step is to plot out the place it will have in the total plan over one, two or three years. That decided, and preparation for the Sunday rather than a retrospective treatment agreed upon, the choice must be made as to which readings. The feasts when all three come together are, in a sense, the easiest case and do not need special attention. But the interrelation of the three readings in Advent and Lent can be obscure and, at some point, surely does require some attention.

A final decision to be made is whether the second readings are to be explored sequentially as they occur—i.e., with the ethical, the doctrinal and the mystical interspersed—or whether readings that cohere around one of these topics should be treated in successive meetings. The lofty exhortations to a Christian life are the most numerous second-reading passages, the easiest to comprehend and of the greatest practical importance to the candidates. These above all should receive major attention, however they are grouped for consideration.

From Catechumenate to the Rest of Life

The way the church proclaims the Bible publicly from week to week is the best clue to its own self-identity. It is a community that thinks these readings best define its existence and mission. No one can be whole-heartedly of this company who recites its creeds and receives its initiatory rites but does not know the apostolic tradition from which they derive in its primary witness.

That is the chief reason for Bible study in lectionary form as the backbone of a catechumenate, however else it may be devised. The second reason is like the first. Catholic life looks to the Bible as its chief wellspring, the church's sacraments being the celebration of God's revealed word contained there. Fruitful celebration of the eucharist and the other life-giving symbols will depend on the Catholic's familiarity with God's word addressed to the church. Will new Catholics be sufficiently at home in the Bible that they will turn to it eagerly and knowledgeably over a lifetime?

All Christians possess the theoretical conviction that they should "read the Bible more," but many do not do so because they find it daunting—and never confide this to anyone else. Even a simple matter such as ignorance of the sequence of the books can put them off. When they do turn to this ancient library, its thought categories often seem so foreign to the Christian lives they are living that they do not persevere as Bible readers. People need above all a sense of achievement in Bible reading. They must once have done it for a sustained period and derived profit and enjoyment from the exercise. There is no better time to acquire this skill than in the training period for the initiatory rite. Only in such case can minimum achievement turn into a lifetime habit.

If Bible reading is already a habit, as it is with some catechumens, they need to learn to read or hear it with Catholic eyes and ears. The fact is that the Bible reveals itself to no one apart from a previous matrix of faith or nonfaith. Even the non-Christian who had never read a line has certain preconceptions about it from hearsay in the culture. Protestant and Evangelical Christians certainly have preconceptions about its meaning. No less is this true of adherents to any of the world's religions or no religion. It is impossible to approach these writings with a mind that is a blank slate on the ideas contained there. Catholicity is an ancient religious tradition that thinks it knows a few things about interpreting the Bible because it received most of it in faith from Israel and, through the apostolic band, composed the rest. As a Western church the Roman tradition will read the Bible in a Western way.

Urban people will miss out on much that rural people will comprehend. The culturally and technologically advanced will miss out on much that those who live closer to the soil and the elements will absorb. Above all, non-Semitic persons exploring this Semitic literature will be puzzled by it time and again.

But a faith community convinced that it holds to the basic faith commitment of the inspired authors of these books, studying them communally, cannot but emerge enriched by the labor.

As Marshal Lyautey said when his orderly demurred at watering the century plant in his garden because it wouldn't bloom for a hundred years, "Then we haven't a moment to lose!"

♦ *Gerard S. Sloyan*

The Lectionary as a Sourcebook of Catechesis in the Catechumenate

A FEW YEARS AGO at the Sunday liturgy, I witnessed the rite of acceptance into the catechumenate at a local parish. One of the candidates was a Chicago-Bears'-Refrigerator-looking man who burst into tears as the priest stretched to mark him with the sign of the cross while saying, "It is Christ himself who now strengthens you with the sign of his love." Afterwards, in conversation with the man, he tried in a somewhat embarrassed fashion to explain what had happened to him. It was this: At that moment, he had experienced a profound sense of being loved by God. The man was coming from a religious tradition in which the acceptance of Jesus as savior was a central focus. For years the preachers had told him that he was loved by God, but it was through this simple rite that he gained insight into that reality.

Formation through the Liturgy

Although the liturgy is principally the worship of God, "it contains much instruction for the faithful" (*Constitution on the Sacred Liturgy*, 33).

Liturgical "instruction" is not didactic, it is intuitive. Liturgical and sacramental rites do not celebrate ideas; they celebrate Christ's presence in our lives, revealed and discovered in the presence of the community gathered in his name. To catechize through the liturgy is to form the catechumen in a liturgical spirituality that is trinitarian and paschal, communal and sacramental, committed to the promotion of the reign of God.[1]

The story of the reception of the catechumen is a poignant example of the kind of catechesis that is envisioned by the Rite of Christian Initiation of Adults; that is, the liturgy and the liturgical rites are primary formative experiences for the catechumen. The lectionary has an important role in this liturgical formation process, but it is not an isolated role. The lectionary is a liturgical book and the proclamation of the word in the liturgy of the word and the breaking open of the word after the Sunday dismissal are one part of the process of liturgical formation.[2]

The catechumenate is "the period of formation in the whole Christian life,"[3] and the RCIA, 75, offers a clear description of the kind of interrelated elements that constitute this formation. First, the catechesis is to be gradual and complete, accommodated to the liturgical year and solidly supported by the celebrations of the word. Second, catechumens are to become familiar with the Christian way of life through the witness and support of sponsors, godparents and the entire Christian community. Third, catechumens are formed by suitable liturgical rites. They may participate in the liturgy of the word at Mass; celebrations of the word of God are to be arranged especially for them, and instruction should always be in the context of prayer. Fourth, the catechumens should also work actively with others to spread the gospel and build up the church. In other words, the catechumen is formed by liturgical rites, by instruction in prayer, by community life and apostolic works.

When we take a careful look at the pastoral formation outlined in paragraph 75 of the RCIA, it becomes apparent that the introduction to the rite offers a different vision than many of us now experience. The initial reaction to this outline of the formation of catechumens may be "Well, isn't that special!"

Then our next response might be "Where is the doctrine?"[4] That's a good question. If we accept that the liturgy and liturgical rites are the primary formative experience, then we realize that a liturgical catechesis reverses our present practice. Currently our catechetical programs are generally organized around theological concepts, and doctrinal teaching has primacy. The concept is developed by drawing upon human experience and appropriate biblical texts. Liturgical experiences become a culmination of the lesson and a reinforcement of the concept.

The Model of Catechesis

The model of catechesis offered in the introduction to the rite takes the mystery of salvation—as it is expressed and effected in the life of this particular catechumen and this particular community—as its starting point. Through word and worship, the catechumen and the community are called to conversion. The focus on a gradual catechesis "accommodated to the liturgical year and solidly supported by celebrations of the word" calls for liturgical catechesis in which the use of the lectionary, a liturgical book, is one aspect of catechesis in the RCIA. Liturgical catechesis points to the seasons of Lent, Triduum and Eastertime as the focal point of the church year. The liturgical year forms and shapes the faith of the catechumen.

Liturgical catechesis demands a process in which catechumens are enabled to reflect upon their daily lives in relationship to the word. The liturgical rites of scrutinies and presentations are a primary catechesis during the lenten period. So is participation in activities that alleviate the plight of the homeless or hungry. The formation described in the introduction is not so much of an innovation as it may appear for it attempts to restore the organic relationship between catechesis and liturgy, a relationship that has virtually been lost since the dissolution of the ancient catechumenate in the early Middle Ages.

In fact, this description of the formation of the catechumens in the RCIA sounds remarkably like the description of catechesis in the National Catechetical Directory, *Sharing the Light of Faith*. This is not surprising since the catechetical directory (115) as well as the "Message to the People of God" (7), issued by the 1977 Synod of Bishops, states that the baptismal catechumenate is the model for all catechesis.[5]

In the understanding of Vatican II and in the official documents published since that time, catechesis is understood as a pastoral ministry of the church, a ministry of the word. The purpose of catechesis is to strengthen and foster the faith of catechumens or of the baptized believers through the light of instruction and through the experience of Christian living.[6] The National Catechetical Directory tells us that catechesis has four tasks: to proclaim the mysteries of faith, to share and foster community, to lead people to worship and prayer and to motivate them to the service of others. Together these four tasks make up the one ministry that we call catechesis. All four are integral to the process of formation in the catechumenate.

Breaking Open the Word

The breaking open of the word in the catechumenal sessions is a significant element in the process of catechesis. Reflection on the word is the link that brings together the proclamation and the celebration of the mystery in signs, actions and words. The liturgical signs and actions "derive their full meaning not simply from their origin in human experience but from the word of God and the economy of salvation, their point of reference" (*Lectionary for Mass*, Introduction [LMIn], 6). Reflection on the word takes place within the framework of the liturgical year and in the context of prayer and worship; it takes place in the midst of the community of believers who are gathered together in response to the word, and the word impels us to act for justice. These elements of message, community, service, prayer and worship are the marks of the Christian.

The lectionary is a liturgical book. Catechesis from the lectionary can never lose sight of that context. The lectionary is proclamation for the purpose of deepening faith and renewing life. The lectionary is not a textbook that one learns. The shared praxis approach that facilitates reflection on the word is good as far as it goes, but it needs to be placed within the framework of liturgical prayer, symbols and rites.

The introduction to the lectionary offers some general principles for the liturgical celebration of the word of God and these same principles apply to catechesis from the lectionary because the Sunday morning dismissal is a prolongation of the liturgy of the word. Each principle tells us something about who we are in relationship to God's word and how we are to be formed in a liturgical spirituality.[7]

We Are a People

The lectionary is the book of the assembly.[8]

> To tell a story of God is to create a world, adopt an attitude, suggest a behavior. But stories are first; we are second. We are born into a community of stories and storytellers. In interpreting our traditional stories of God we find out who we are and what we must do.[9]

The "stories are first; we are second." The assembly is constituted by the proclamation of the word. Two stories are foundational to the understanding of ourselves as an assembly: the event at Sinai in which the ragtag group of Hebrew people entered into a covenant with the Lord God and became a people, a holy nation, and the death/resurrection of Jesus, the new covenant that formed a new people.

In the Sunday assembly the community is called together to share a common faith and a common vision. In the midst of this assembly, the proclamation of the word offers us a way of understanding our lives and our world from the perspective of our covenant relationship with God. It also offers us a way of entering into relationship with Christ, because Christ is present in the assembly and in his word. In the gathering and in the proclamation of the word we make manifest the Christ who is already present. The readings call us to identify ourselves as the concrete sign of Christ in the world. In the assembly we are no longer simply a group of individuals but we are a people in whom Christ is present.

Once when I asked the students to give an example of a time in which they realized that they were "more" than individuals, one student told about being with his wife during the birth of their child. He said, "There we were, Rose and I, husband and wife. Then the baby came and we were a family!" He hesitated and then said, "I can't tell you what it was like but it was a terrific experience!"

"Whenever the church, gathered by the Holy Spirit for liturgical celebration, announces and proclaims the word of God, it has the experience of being a new people in whom the covenant made in the past is fulfilled." (LMIn, 7). The "stories of God" are our stories; we are the people in whom the covenant made in the past is fulfilled. We will probably never be able to explain what it is like to be a new people; we can only experience it.

The word that is broken open in the catechumenal session is the word that is proclaimed in the midst of the Sunday assembly. Reflection on the word must lead the catechumen to a deeper sense of the communal reality of the church. The lectionary is by its very nature community oriented. Reflection that leads to a "Jesus and I" spirituality misunderstands and misuses the lectionary.

We Are a People of Promise and Memory

As we remember God's saving deeds in history, we are assured of God's saving promise in our history. God's infinite love for us is the reference point for all that we do. The word proclaimed in the liturgy is always a living, active word through the power of the Spirit. It expresses God's love "that never fails in its effectiveness toward us" (LMIn, 4).

"The liturgical celebration, based primarily on the word of God and sustained by it, becomes a new event and enriches the word itself with new meaning and power." (LMIn, 3) Christians are a people of memory and the focus of our memorial is the death and resurrection of Jesus. To remember is to enter into the paschal mystery and in each of our Sunday celebrations to recall and renew this event as we recall and renew our baptism into new life. We bring our own experience of dying and rising—of suffering and possibility, of sin and forgiveness, of alienation and reconciliation, of despair and hope—and join it to the saving action of Christ. The liturgical year begins and ends in the paschal event. Every feast and every season is related to the mystery of Easter; every eucharistic celebration actualizes this saving event.

The fundamental paradigm of the Christian life is the paschal mystery, the event through which the most profound mysteries of our own life find meaning. In the catechesis through the lectionary, the "new meaning and power" of the word must be continually explored and appropriated. At times, perhaps because it is a familiar approach, there is a tendency to look at the liturgical readings as a kind of year-long biography of Christ that simply correlates the events in the life of

Jesus with the liturgical year. This chronological method turns Christ into a historical figure of the past and relegates the mystery of Christ to separate and distinct events. The word of God can never be reduced to a past event because each time the word is proclaimed it re-creates that event. When Jesus says to Peter, "Who do you say that I am?" (the central question of Mark's gospel), it is a question addressed to each of us now. "Who do you say that I am?" The word of God proclaimed in the lectionary makes us a people of memory, calling to mind what God has done, is doing now and will continue to do in our life.

We Are a People of Time

The liturgical year is the framework in which the catechumen is formed. The proclaimed word enables the catechumen to enter into the mystery of Christ from a particular perspective because in the liturgical celebration the texts go beyond a purely exegetical meaning and assume a sacramental meaning in their liturgical proclamation. In the reading from the Gospel of John for the Third Sunday of Lent (Cycle A), for example, the story of the woman at the well, from an exegetical view, concerns the gift of grace and does not explicitly involve a sacramental dimension. Nor do the readings from Exodus and from Paul. Nevertheless, the most ancient tradition grouped these three texts as the basis of the liturgical catechesis of the catechumens preparing for baptism in the Easter Vigil.[10] The lenten context of the readings gives them powerful baptismal significance for the catechumen. The same comment can be made of the readings for the fourth (the man born blind) and fifth Sundays of Lent (the raising of Lazarus). Through the readings, the baptismal symbols of water, light and life are broken open for the catechumens so that they may enter more deeply into the mystery contained in these themes.

The readings are given a particular focus in the context of the liturgical season. The readings for Advent prepare us for the coming of Christ in the end time. We are able to live in hope and expectation because the word became flesh and dwells among us. Lent centers on conversion and the process of initiation. Eastertime reminds us that the whole life of the church arises out of the paschal mystery. The resurrection is the event that establishes the church, and Pentecost underlines the mission of the church to build up the body of Christ through the gifts of the Spirit. The readings for Ordinary Time provide us with a picture of Jesus and of the church from the perspective of a particular evangelist. In Ordinary Time the word of God is addressed to believers in a kind of continuous present. The readings help us to look at our life and to see the extraordinary in what is ordinary. In reflecting on the word in catechumenal sessions, the liturgical context that brings interpretation to the reading needs to be kept in mind so that the faith of the church may shape and form the mind and heart of the catechumen.

We Are a Pilgrim People

The lectionary with its three-year Sunday cycle of readings reminds us that we are a people always on a journey. Growth in faith is a lifelong process; the choice and sequence of the readings aim to give the faithful an ever-deepening perception of the faith that they profess and of the history of salvation as it unfolds in their lives. Growth in faith is gradual, and the framers of the lectionary were cognizant of that. Even though we hear the same stories again and again, we are not the same people. We change; our lives change, but it is always "who we are" that God calls to life in the liturgical proclamation of the word.

We Are a People of Mission

In the hearing of God's word, the church is built up and grows (LMIn, 7). The scriptures are not only stories of God's faithfulness to God's people, not only a tradition that gives us a sense of who we are, but they are also challenges. We hear the word and it is a mirror in which we look at our life. We are called as a people of covenant to commit ourselves to the word of God made flesh in Christ and to endeavor to conform our way of life to that word. We listen to the prophets turn the people away from the worship of idols: What idols do we need to turn away from in our life? We feel the confusion and anger of the elder brother in the story of the prodigal son: Who is the family member or friend with whom we need to be reconciled? God whose word is shared with us awaits our response. In the power of the Spirit, we who are hearers of the word are called to be "doers of the word" (LMIn, 6).

Once, when teaching a class on reconciliation, I asked the students to reflect upon the parable of the prodigal son. Because many in the class were drama majors, I asked them to put the parable into "scenes" that indicated the main aspects of the story. My aim was to show that these aspects—turning away, remorse, turning back and welcome— would parallel the process of the sacrament of penance. As the students were working, I noticed that one had simply crumpled up the paper and thrown it on the floor. I went to her and in my best Rogerian manner asked if something was the matter. She responded that she hated the story. After class, she told me that her sister, strung out on drugs, had disappeared. Her parents were heartbroken and went to great lengths to find their daughter. The student herself gave up a wonderful opportunity in order to stay home with her parents. One day when she came home from school, she saw that all the lights were on at her house and that cars belonging to her brothers were parked outside. She began to run, convinced that something had happened to her parents. When she opened the door, her mother, full of happiness, came running to her to tell her that her sister had come home. Her mother said, "I thought she was dead! She's here, she's OK!" The girl saw that the table was set as if it were a holiday. Then her sister came into the room. The student said, "I went over to her and slapped her! Then I went upstairs and got my things and I have not been back since. That's why I hate that story." The parable has the power to challenge and to call for a decision. It can be accepted or rejected. In this situation, forgiveness needs to be given and to be sought. The parable initiates a process and hopefully in time it will bring about a transformation.

We Are a Eucharistic People

The breaking open of the word is always directed to the breaking of the bread. "The celebration of Mass in which the word is heard and the eucharist is offered and received, forms but one single act of divine worship." (LMIn, 10) In the word of God the covenant is announced; in the eucharist the new and everlasting covenant is renewed. At times some catechumens may, because of the deep satisfaction found in sharing the word, see the celebration of the word in the catechumenal session as an end point. (Catechists may at times feel the same way.) For the catechumen and for those whose pastoral situation limits their participation in the eucharist, the belief in Christ's real presence in their gathering and in the word is strengthened but must lead to an anticipation and a longing for the fullness of the sign of their unity in Christ. The eucharist is an action, an action of all those gathered together in service of the word. The catechumen must be led to see that word and eucharistic action are contained and completed in one another or they will begin to have a distorted appreciation of both the one and the other.

The lectionary can never be separated from liturgical catechesis. Together they are constitutive of a liturgical spirituality and prayer that build a foundation for the catechumen's spiritual life as a fully initiated Christian.

Sunday by Sunday

The gradual unfolding of the scripture Sunday by Sunday in its proclamation and reflection in the catechumenate session gives the catechumen a powerful means of entering into the Christian life. Those of us who have prepared children and adults for participation in the sacraments know that one of the greatest obstacles to understanding and participation is the lack of context. People simply do not have the biblical background to understand the language of sacrament, which is permeated by themes from both the Hebrew and Christian scriptures. The dominant liturgical symbols—particularly the preeminent symbol of the assembly itself—of water, wine, oil, bread, light and darkness, the cross and the laying on of hands have no point of reference. Furthermore, most people see little connection between their worship and their life. To catechize from the liturgy and from the lectionary is to build up a lexicon of image and sign that enables catechumens to name more fully their own experience of God and to enter more deeply into God's presence. The experience and the reflection on that experience in terms of one's life and in the power of the Spirit calls the catechumens to try "to conform their way of life to what they celebrate in the liturgy and to bring to the celebration of the liturgy all that they do in life" (LMIn, 6).

Will doctrine be taught? Would a catechumen who seriously reflects upon the woman at the well not come to a profound understanding of the meaning of grace, both as a theological concept and a profound personal reality? Or who reflects upon the disciples on the road to Emmaus without coming to some understanding of the presence of Christ in the word and in the breaking of bread? Can one pray "through Jesus Christ, your Son, who lives and reigns with you and the Holy Spirit, one God for ever and ever" without coming to an awareness of the life of the Trinity? Will not many questions arise out of the catechumen's own reflection? Doctrine will be learned as it is lived and experienced in the life of the church in the liturgical year.

The reflection on the word will raise many questions for the catechumen. Other weekly or biweekly sessions apart from the Sunday dismissal could address some doctrinal or historical issues that concern the catechumen or that are a part of Catholic Christian formation. These sessions could also attend to some of the inadequacies of the present lectionary[11] with regard to the minimal emphasis given to the creation and covenant narratives,[12] to the arrangement of readings that does not give an equal and independent place to the Hebrew scriptures,[13] and to the frequency and value of references to women in the lectionary.[14] This catechetical instruction should take place within the framework of prayer, particularly liturgical prayer, and should include some liturgical action, such as the signing with the cross, the laying on of hands or a blessing.

For Life

It is necessary to keep the RCIA within the perspective of a lifelong process and not expect the rite to accomplish a total formation. The RCIA gives special attention to a particular moment in the spiritual journey of those seeking initiation into the Catholic Christian community; it is the task of the Christian community to insure that this process of formation continues long beyond the period of mystagogia.

Yes, it must be recognized that the word of God does not always "stir the hearts of the hearers with the same power. Always, however,

Christ is present in his word. As he carries out the mystery of salvation, he sanctifies us and offers the Father perfect worship" (LMIn, 4).

◆ *Catherine Dooley, OP*

Notes

1. A helpful work on the relationship of liturgy and spirituality is Kevin Irwin, *Liturgy, Prayer and Spirituality* (New York: Paulist Press, 1984).

2. See Karen Hinman Powell, "The Lectionary As a Source Book for Catechesis in the Catechumenate," *Breaking Open the Word of God: Resources for Using the Lectionary for Catechesis in the RCIA, Cycle A,* Karen Hinman Powell and Joseph Sinwell, editors (New York: Paulist Press, 1986), 10–13, for an excellent method of preparation for the Sunday morning dismissal session.

3. The pastoral formation outlined in the RCIA is based on the Vatican II decree on the church's missionary activity, *Ad gentes,* 4, which states that the candidate who has received from God the gift of faith in Christ through the church should be admitted with liturgical rites to the catechumenate that is not a mere exposition of dogmatic truths and norms of morality but a period of formation in the whole Christian life, an apprenticeship of sufficient duration during which the disciples will be joined to Christ their teacher.

4. James Dunning addresses the question of doctrine in "Catechesis through the Lectionary: Soft on Doctrine or Strong on Faith," *Breaking Open the Word of God: Resources for Using the Lectionary for Catechesis in the RCIA, Cycle B*, Karen Hinman Powell and Joseph Sinwell, editors (New York: Paulist Press, 1987), 3–8.

5. Synod of Bishops, 1977, "Message to the People of God," *The Living Light* 15 (Spring 1978), 86–97; *Sharing the Light of Faith: National Catechetical Directory for Catholics of the United States* (Washington DC: United States Catholic Conference, 1979), 115, states that RCIA provides a norm for catechetical and liturgical practice for initiation into the church.

6. *Christus Dominus*, 14; Code of Canon Law, c. 773, goes beyond the description of catechesis in *Christus Dominus* by adding "the experience of Christian living" to emphasize that faith is also nurtured in an informal way through interaction with the community.

7. See Mary Collins, "Liturgy," *The New Dictionary of Theology* (Wilmington DE: Michael Glazier, 1987), 594–96, for the characteristics of liturgical prayer.

8. See Gerard Sloyan, "The Bible As the Book of the Church," *Worship* 60 (January 1986), 9–21.

9. John Shea, *Stories of God* (Chicago: Thomas More Press, 1978), 9.

10. Thierry Maertens, "History and Function of the Three Great Pericopes," Johannes

Wagner, editor, *Adult Baptism and the Catechumenate,* Concilium 22 (New York: Paulist Press, 1967), 51–56.

11. For a critical look at the selection of readings included in the present lectionary, see Gerard Sloyan, "The Lectionary As a Context for Interpretation," *Interpretation* (1977), 131–38.

12. Mary Collins, "Devotion and Renewal Movements: Spiritual Cousins of the Liturgy," *Called to Prayer* (Collegeville: The Liturgical Press, 1986), 66–67.

13. Herman Wegman, "Significant Effects of Insignificant Changes," *Liturgy: A Creative Tradition*, Concilium 162, M. Collins and D. Power, editors, (New York: Seabury Press, 1983), 56–57; Jim Wilde, "The Lectionary: Some Problems and Remedies," *Catechumenate: A Journal of Christian Initiation* (March 1987), 25–30.

14. Margaret Procter-Smith, "Images of Women in the Lectionary," in *Women Invisible in Church and Theology*, Concilium 182, E. Schussler-Fiorenza and M. Collins, editors, (Edinburgh: T & T Clark, 1985), 51–62.

Prebaptismal and Postbaptismal Catechesis for Adults

THE PRESIDENT OF A PARISH COUNCIL put the following in the parish newsletter:

> I have a friend named Henry who taught me all the Polish I know, including most of my jokes. In his own way Henry was a philosopher. One of his best sayings in a time of stress, when people were getting lost in the details, was: "Don't worry about nothin'. Nothin's gonna be all right!"

In other words, get to the "somethin's." Take care of "somethin's," and "nothin's" will take care of themselves.

From Religious "Nothin's" to "Somethin's"

Some claim that the "somethin's" of adult catechesis have moved from the pabulum of memorized texts in catechisms to the fine fare of scripture study or the theology of Vatican II. They offer classes with brilliant lectures or groovy audiovisuals. They wonder why no one comes.

Meanwhile, outside their classrooms "somethin'" is happening. A marriage flounders. A child dies. A job runs out of gas and grinds to a halt. An old man smiles someone back to life. A daughter comes home. A friend forces open a shell. A loved one wakes his beloved with a kiss. These are "somethin's" of adult life; and if scripture study or theology ignore these, adults vote with their feet and exit brilliant lectures about religion cut off from life.

Theologian Karl Rahner claimed the church's life is dominated by "ritualism, legalism, administration and a boring and resigned spiritual mediocrity." He said, "We must admit that we are to a terrifying extent a spiritually lifeless church."[1]

Contributing to lifelessness and listlessness is catechesis, in all its forms including homilies, separated from life. It is often a catechesis that adopts an educational model (education at its worst), lecturing information rather than inviting to transformation and conversion.

Elsewhere Rahner suggests that we should catechize not for religious facts but for spirituality and mysticism. "The Christian of the future will be a mystic or will not be a Christian at all."[2] Don't fear those words "spirituality" and "mysticism." By mysticism he does not mean extraordinary visions but discovery and union with God who is present in the very ordinary "somethin's" of marriage, job, friendship and love. In such ordinary times made extraordinary we meet our God. Theologian John Shea says: "There are moments which, although they occur within the everyday confines of human living, take on larger meaning. They cut through to something deeper; they demand a hearing. Whatever it is, we sense we have undergone something that has touched upon the normally dormant but always present relationship to God."[3] Catechesis for mysticism invites people into those moments. Much of adult education flounders because it takes schooling and not this kind of mysticism and spirituality as its umbrella.

Into this spiritually lifeless scene enter the Rite of Christian Initiation of Adults. For new Christians this catechumenate offers "a spiritual journey" (cf. RCIA, 5). Spirituality is the lens through which we see everything in the catechumenate. Everything has to do with experiencing the good news of God's presence and love in our lives. That is the lens for new Christians. It should be the lens for all Christians. The baptized do not join the catechumenate for renewal or enrichment, but the catechesis that they deserve is enlivened by the same dynamics envisioned in the catechumenate.

In exploring those dynamics I shall begin at the end. The final period of catechesis is mystagogy—the 50 days of Eastertime leading to Pentecost, 50 days of savoring the mysteries of our dying/rising in Jesus. It is postbaptismal catechesis. If we look at the end, we discover what leads to that end. We do prebaptismal catechesis in light of what kind of Christian adults we hope come out of Easter waters filled with the Spirit who renews the face of the earth.

Postbaptismal Catechesis: To Eat as Jesus Did

In 1973 the United States bishops published a pastoral letter entitled "To Teach as Jesus Did."[4] The RCIA suggests that, if we teach as Jesus did, there is no more important result than learning to eat as Jesus did. The postbaptismal catechesis of the 50 days of mystagogy is precisely eating at the Sunday eucharists (cf. RCIA, 247). What does that mean? How did Jesus eat? How does Jesus teach by eating?

Scripture scholar Xavier Leon-Dufour claims that the scriptures tell two tales about how Jesus eats his final meal.[5] The first is in the synoptic gospels and in Paul who tells us Jesus' words, "This bread is my body broken for you; this cup is the new covenant of my blood shed for you." Too much theology focuses only on the bread and cup. We forget the "broken" and "shed." We forget that when we eat and drink that bread and cup, *we* become body broken and blood shed for all our sisters and brothers. We forget that the last supper was like all the meals Jesus ate and all the meals his Father eats—meals that offer life and healing for those most rejected and alien, e.g., the woman "who had a bad name in the town" (Luke 7:36-50), prodigal sons and daughters (Luke 15:11-32), Zacchaeus, the puny tax collector (Luke 19:1-10), motley crowds at wedding feasts (Matthew 22:1-10), gentiles finally welcome at Jewish tables (Mark 8:1-10), all brought to a climax by broken disciples who recognize the Lord in shared brokenness when they break bread (Luke 24:13-35). At those meals Jesus catechized, not by lecturing about love but by eating with love. He "did it by doing it" and he told us to "do this in memory of me."

John knew that. Therefore, his version of the supper doesn't even quote Jesus' words about broken body and shed blood. He tells us that

Jesus did what he always did at meals: wash feet. This meal is not just consuming bread and wine. It is being consumed by love of neighbor—washing feet—body broken and blood shed that others might live, especially the most alien and unloved. In John's gospel he clearly "did it by doing it," and he commands us to do the same: "I have set an example for you, so that you will do just what I have done for you" (John 13:15).

Therefore, for new Christians postbaptismal catechesis is really "doing" these Easter eucharists. *Doing* eucharist, however, is much more than attending, receiving or being at eucharist. When we use that language we give ourselves away. We say that eucharist is just the priest doing something to bread and wine. Bread and wine become objects, things on a table, commodities, rather than our sharing as a community in Jesus' broken body and shed blood given for the life of the world. When that happens, we have worship without witness, celebration without service, liturgy cut off from life, supper without the washing of feet, religion without the "somethin's" of people's lives.

If we eat as Jesus did, however, we literally give ourselves away. In our marriages, families, friendships, work, neighborhoods, communities, with the hungry, thirsty, naked, prisoner and stranger (cf. Matthew 25), with the poor, the captives, the blind and the oppressed (cf. Luke 4) we give ourselves away as eucharist, as body broken and blood shed for justice, compassion, healing and reconciliation. We do this in memory of him.

That is why the RCIA says that postbaptismal catechesis for new Christians is "meditation on the gospel, sharing in the eucharist and doing the works of charity" (RCIA, 244).

Meditation on the gospel is what they did throughout their prebaptismal catechesis. That meditation is not primarily about texts. It is about life, "somethin's," stories of lives seen in light of stories of scripture.

The new Christians also learn what it means to eat as Jesus did not only by "sharing in the eucharist" but by reflecting at those eucharists on what happened to them at the Easter Vigil. The early church did sacramental catechesis after Easter. They relied upon the powerful symbol of the great vigil to immerse the candidates in the meaning of baptism/confirmation/eucharist. So we ask the neophytes, what did they experience—at the fire, in the procession, during the word, at the bathing, in the anointing, at the exchange of peace, during the eating and drinking, with each other, with their godparents, with the assembly, with their God? What does all this mean? What does it mean to become and to live as the body of Christ given for the world in "works of charity" by washing feet?

The United States bishops ask that new Catholic Christians meet in small groups with other Christians for one year after initiation to continue to meditate on the scriptures. In a land in which Christianity is becoming increasingly countercultural, in which the soaps have their version of "one life to live," "days of our lives" and "another world," the bishops suggest that gospel spirituality is still fragile for our new members. They need the support of scripture shared by believers who can assure them that poverty of spirit, fullness of mercy, thirst for justice, purity of heart and peacemaking are the best life to live (Matthew 5).

This catechumenal model of postbaptismal catechesis holds true for all Christians. The normal fare for all Christians is meditation on the scriptures of the liturgical year Sunday after Sunday with the help of homilies that connect our stories to the great stories of the good news. Those stories bring all Christians to the eucharistic table where they become body broken and blood shed. They leave that table to do the "works of charity," to wash feet, to discover Jesus where he said he would be: in the hungry, thirsty, naked, prisoner and stranger (Matthew 25). That also *is* catechesis, to walk the Way and not just talk the Way, to learn about Christ by following Christ.

Research suggests that if people are to come to depth of faith, not just new Christians but all Christians need to meet from time to time in small communities of faith to break open the scriptures and make connections with their lives. The model is not a theology class but the communal spiritual journey of the catechumenate that sees conversion as an ongoing journey to and from the table of the eucharist. It is not the teacher-pupil relationship of the classroom but shared wisdom and experience like that of Alcoholics Anonymous or any 12-step program.

Prebaptismal Catechesis: Preparing to Eat as Jesus Did

If postbaptismal catechesis is learning to eat as Jesus did, everything we do before the baptism of adults (and everything we do for baptized adults who don't know how to eat) is to prepare for that kind of meal. The catechumenate offers that in three periods of prebaptismal catechesis: evangelization during the precatechumenate, catechesis during the catechumenate and retreat during Lent. The last will be dealt with at the conclusion of this presentation.

Precatechumenate: Evangelization with a Redhot Iron. George Bernanos said: "The Word of God! It is a redhot iron. And you who teach want to take it up with tongs for fear of burning yourself. Why don't you grasp it with both hands?"[6] Precatechumenate catechesis grasps that iron and proclaims scripture, scripture and more scripture.

The goal of the precatechumenate is evangelization through the scriptures which leads to initial faith and conversion into the mystery of God's love (RCIA, 36, 37). Unlike Paul VI who saw evangelization as everything that the church does to proclaim good news, the catechumenate limits evangelization to the first hearing of that message.

This form of catechesis has all the excitement and enthusiasm of new beginnings. A person may have heard about *the* faith for some time. Too often we limit faith to faith as cognitive content rather than faith as relationship. Biblical faith is personal relationship with God expressed in attitudes, feelings, beliefs, worship, responsibilities. Faith dies without some expression, just as the relationship of marriage dies without intercourse (in the broadest sense: all the ways that two persons in love give themselves to each other). The problem is that we can receive the results of someone else's faith without the relationship that gave birth to those results. We can mouth doctrines and perform rituals of a tradition without personal experience of God's love. Evangelization offers that experience of love. That is exciting.

That happens when we invite people to put themselves into scripture stories. They see themselves as the people loved by God. "Yes! We are the people freed from slavery and called to the promised land. We are the people returning home from exile. We are the prodigal sons or daughters embraced by the Father. We are the workers in the vineyard overpaid. We are the lost sheep carried home. We are Lazarus unbound. We are the broken ones who find the Lord in breaking bread." Evangelization is connecting scripture with "somethin's" in our lives.

If evangelization has the excitement of new beginnings, the best scriptures are the most exciting stories, the hottest iron. Walter Brueggemann insists that we need to relate all scripture to what he calls the "primal stories": that most simple story at the heart of biblical faith, the most important story we know, the one before which every other story is judged. For Israel that is the events surrounding the exodus. For Christians it is the dying-rising of Jesus. These are the real "somethin's" for Jews and Christians. The "expanded story" is a more elaborate presentation of the primal story. For Israel that might include all the great journey stories of the Hebrew scriptures. For Christians it is an entire gospel.[7] For new Christians evangelization in the precatechumenate normally will proclaim scriptures which are closest to the primal story.

What is true for scripture is true for all the content of catechesis: All must be rooted in the experience of that primal story of God's love in the exodus and in the paschal mystery. One author states, "What is learned is no more and no less than the love *of* God *through* Jesus Christ and *in* the Holy Spirit. All the doctrines of Christianity are but explications of that one statement."[8] The unbaptized who join a church are often interested in doctrines/practices that make that church different. *The* Catholic difference, shared with other sacramental churches, is primarily on the level of experience, not doctrine. Catholics experience God in the "somethin's" of their lives: in people and events. That shows up in other Catholic differences: saints and Mary, seven sacraments, not just two, 70 times seven sacramentals with smells and bells, popes and structures. Catholics live in a sacramental world where they experience God incarnate, in the flesh, in all creation. We risk learning the results without the experience. That becomes idolatry, fundamentalism, ritualism, legalism, the spiritual mediocrity decried by Rahner. Doctrines, rubrics and laws become gods.

If that has happened for the baptized, they need the same evangelization offered to the unbaptized. A Gallup study says that among the major churches, Catholics are least likely to agree that "God loves you a great deal" and that they have a personal relationship with God.[9] They need to grasp the redhot iron of God's word and make their own the exciting good news of the primal story.

Indeed, with unbaptized and baptized we explore our rich biblical and postbiblical tradition but always with an invitation to experience

God's presence and love in the ways that our ancestors in faith found the primal stories of exodus and pasch in their lives and times. The ultimate goal is always to bring their stories and ours to the eucharistic table during mystagogy and to continue the exodus and the dying/rising of Jesus in his body and blood given for the world today.

Catechumenate: Catechesis Echoes the Word.

A loose translation of catechesis would be "to echo the word," literally to resound the good news again and again. If evangelization is the first hearing, if evangelization means beginnings, catechesis means growth, ongoing nurture, deepening our relationship with God in faith.

Note that catechesis is not mere instruction, theology, abstract information or Rahner's "spiritual mediocrity of forms without faith." In the precatechumenate, some tolerate evangelization aimed at head, heart and hands. In the catechumenate period, however, they say it's now time for doctrinal beef. It's cortex time. Never. Like evangelization, catechesis is always about faith, conversion, transformation and never mere information.

The catechumenal vision of prebaptismal catechesis is outlined in RCIA, 75. It echoes the vision of the United States Catechetical Directory that sees catechesis as: ministry of the word, building community, worship and witness.[10] The RCIA speaks of exploring scripture and doctrine, entering the life of the community in prayer and action, celebrating liturgies, and apostolic witness in the world. Both approaches invite not just the cortex but the whole person into deeper faith.

Exploring Scripture and Doctrine. Because it is a *rite* of initiation, the context for catechesis is rites. The place is not classroom but church. If possible, the time is not weeknight but Sunday liturgy of the word. The books are not catechisms (have them as aids on your shelf) but lectionary. Because Gerard Sloyan and Catherine Dooley treat lectionary-based catechesis in this volume, I shall limit myself to two remarks. First, the process of breaking open the word is the same as that described above under evangelization. Second, the United States bishops suggest that most people need one year of catechesis in the catechumenate period. That would mean they could explore the primal story in one expanded story, the scriptures of one liturgical year.

Regarding doctrine, I share the concern of those who complain about the dearth of religious knowledge. In response, however, some want to change homilies back to doctrinal, topical sermons; and they want catechumenates to be inquiry classes. The catechumenate is about initiation, about the basics. It uses quality terms, not quantity terms, about doctrine: "suitable, appropriate, profound."

We respond to all of the catechumens' questions about Catholic life and doctrine, but we avoid the trap of fundamentalism and legalism by connecting doctrine/practice with our life of faith and experience of God. Postbaptismal catechesis for a lifetime can explore all the implications of that experience. In the catechumenate period we are about the basics. The basics are not doctrine and law but love by God and for God and neighbor. When that emerges into creeds, codes and cults, the liturgy shows what is basic. It has two presentations of our tradition. It gives the catechumens the creed and the Lord's Prayer. Those are basic. Cardinal Ratzinger, head of the Congregation of the Doctrine of the Faith, says: "The entire exposition on faith is organized around four basic elements: the creed, the Lord's Prayer, the commandments and the sacraments. This is the basis of the life of the Christian."[11]

Community Life

Cardinal Newman said: "The general principles of any study you may learn by books at home; but the detail, the color, the tone, the air, the life which makes it live in us, you must catch all these from those in whom it lives already."[12] The unbaptized meet the baptized: Ethel with cancer, Joe who coordinates the food bank, Jennifer and David who tell of their marriage, Margaret who prays the rosary, Pete who prays with a charismatic prayer group, Dan who prays the liturgy of the hours with a group, Nancy who helps families and victims of AIDS, John who helps people get better housing. If they are to be the body of Christ given for the life of the world, they learn from that body how to be that body.

Liturgical Celebrations

"Where e're the Catholic sun doth shine, there's music and laughter and good red wine. At least I've heard them tell it so, 'Benedicamus Domino.'" That Belloc paraphrase is especially true of the galaxy of rites and liturgies offered by the catechumenate: welcoming, receiving cross and scriptures, blessing and exorcising, calling and signing names, praying and singing, bathing, laying on hands, anointing with oil, touching, washing with water, eating bread and drinking wine.

James Michael Lee complains that too much of religious education is verbal and cognitive. Too often we identify that as the only content. Lee insists that there is other content, most of which is more effective than words and concepts in coming to faith. Along with other scientists in various fields, Lee insists that feelings and attitudes are affective content. There is nonverbal content (e.g., the presence of the catechist and the group or community), unconscious content (explored with Freud and Jung), process content (the way we catechize through processes of experiencing, thinking, valuing and the methods we use that communicate respect or disrespect). His most important content is life-style. To *do* faith, to let faith emerge in behavior is to grow in faith.[13]

If Lee is correct, I cannot imagine a richer source of catechetical content than the well-celebrated liturgies of the catechumenate, splendid with robust signs and symbols, gesture and vesture. Before, during and after these liturgies we use the same principle of mystagogy that unpacks the Easter Vigil. We ask the candidates what they experienced and what it means. What has this celebration communicated about discipleship, election, the cross, God's word, community, witness, sin, grace, God's love?

Apostolic Witness

If Lee is correct when he claims that the most important content of catechesis is what he calls life-style, then witness *during* the catechumenate period is the most important form of catechesis. It is also the most ignored. If our new members disappear after Easter, if they have little sense of being baptized for witness and mission, the malady probably began in the catechumenate period. By inviting them into mission as part of their formation we communicate that we are baptized into body broken and blood shed for the life of the world.

Theologian Mark Searle says: "We do not first know Christ and then follow him. Like the disciples we come to know *by* following him." To know Jesus is to follow Jesus. The Hebrew word for word is *dabar*, which is better translated as word–deed. To believe God's word is to do God's word. The truth is to do the truth.

Therefore, we invite catechumens into mission. After their baptism, with a small group we shall support them in their mission for at least a year. The preference is not to invite them into an ecclesial ministry, e.g., liturgical ministries, catechetical ministries or even catechumenal ministries. We prefer to help them continue to connect the scriptures with their life in family, work, neighborhood and world where the reign of God happens. The same is true for the catechumenate period, but during this time we might invite them into groups active in social concerns and the corporal works of mercy so that they might discover Christ in his broken body.

For the baptized, we need to explore the implications of this vision of the catechumenate. What if sacramental formation of parents and families at times of infant baptism, or first eucharist, or reconciliation, or what if marriage preparation or ministry at the time of a death exposed people to word, community celebration and witness?

Lent: Retreat into the Desert

For the unbaptized the catechumenate calls for an intense period of "spiritual recollection" during Lent (RCIA, 138). The catechesis of the catechumenate period continues, but the environment now is clearly a six-week retreat preparing for initiation. The gospel of the first Sunday sets the tone by sending us into the desert.

Because the focus is on spiritual preparation, the ministry of spiritual direction becomes even more important. Candidates might meet with their director weekly. If possible, candidates might make a formal weekend retreat, perhaps with people who experienced the catechumenate in the past. They are invited to participate in whatever the parish is doing for Lent, including prayer and fasting. Some candidates have organized social concerns projects during Lent for the parish.

The scrutinies on the third, fourth and fifth Sundays of Lent, with their rich images of woman thirsting, man blind and Lazarus bound, are powerful catecheses for both the unbaptized and the entire community. The scrutinies "uncover, then heal all that is weak and strengthen all that is good" (RCIA, 141). In strong litanies we name not just the sins of individuals but the sins of the world, social sin in which we are enmeshed and ensnared. We lay on hands to exorcise those evil spirits and call forth the Holy Spirit. We cannot face those demons alone. The entire community promises to live not by those evil spirits but by the Holy Spirit of justice, compassion, reconciliation and peace.

The final prebaptismal catechesis is the great Triduum. Along with the entire community, candidates enter the dying/rising of the Lord and we are back where we started—back to mystagogy with people who have become eucharist, become body broken and blood shed for the sisters and brothers. We begin again at the end. Postbaptismal catechesis for a lifetime invites new and old Christians to take all their "somethin's" and make them eucharist so that all might eat as Jesus did.

◆ *James B. Dunning*

Notes

1. Karl Rahner, *The Shape of the Church to Come* (NY: Seabury Press, 1972), 23.

2. Karl Rahner, "Theology and Spirituality of Pastoral Work in the Parish," *Theological Investigations* 19 (NY: Crossroads, 1983), 99.

3. John Shea, *An Experience Named Spirit* (Chicago: Thomas More Press, 1983), 98.

4. "To Teach as Jesus Did" (Washington DC: United States Catholic Conference, 1973).

5. Xavier Léon-Dufour, *Sharing the Eucharist Bread* (NY: Paulist Press, 1987), 283-85.

6. Cited by Pierre-André Liége, "The Ministry of the Word: From Kerygma to Catechesis," *Lumen Vitae* 17 (1962), 21-36.

7. Walter Brueggemann, *The Bible Makes Sense* (Winona MN: St. Mary's Press, 1977).

8. Charles Hefling, *Why Doctrines?* (NY: Cowley Press, 1984), 69.

9. George Gallup, Jr. and Jim Castelli, *The American Catholic People: Their Beliefs, Practices and Values* (Garden City: Doubleday and Company, 1987), 193.

10. *Sharing the Light of Faith* (Washington DC: United States Catholic Conference, 1979), 213.

11. Cited by Michael J. Wrenn, "Religious Education at the Crossroads," in *Religious Education and the Future,* Dermot Lane, editor (NY: Paulist Press, 1986), 47.

12. F. X. Connolly, editor, *A Newman Reader* (Garden City: Image Books, 1964), 181.

13. James Michael Lee, *The Content of Religious Instruction: A Social Science Approach* (Birmingham: Religious Education Press, 1985).

Catechizing Families with Infants and Preschoolers

A T THE CELEBRATION OF BAPTISM, parents stand before the Christian community, asking for support as they publicly affirm their decision to raise their children in the faith. The presence of adult ministers at baptism is a visible pledge that we will walk with the children in hope and love, for it is into the adult community of faith that children are baptized. How seriously do we take the promises that our prayer and presence make at baptism? How can we as parish and individuals help create and sustain an environment where the commitment of parents and children can grow?

Baptism is the public celebration of the beginning of life in the church. From the moment of birth the child has felt the presence and care of God through parents, family and neighbors. Now that experience is broadened to include the Christian community gathered in worship. Parishes are recognizing the need to nurture parents' commitment to the risen Christ. What are some practical ways this can be done? Where do parishes begin?

Baptism policies for most dioceses in the United States speak of appropriate catechesis opportunities for parents wishing to baptize their infants and young children. Practically, what can this look like in a local church? Each worshiping community reflects a unique aspect of the body of Christ on earth. Therefore, each parish's baptism preparation, celebration and follow-up catechetical opportunities for parents and their infants, toddlers and young children will be a unique expression of the love of that church. Sharing experiences from various parishes can enrich all of us and can spark the creativity of parish staffs whose responsibility it is to ensure that *there is an intentional design or plan* for baptism in each local church.

Baptismal catechesis is threefold: preparation, celebration and follow-up through the years of infancy amd early childhood. In exploring these three aspects of catechesis, it is essential that the family be our primary focus. Young parents preparing to celebrate a first child's baptism have needs somewhat different from parents who may be preparing for a third or fourth child or parents of an adopted child. Parish staffs need to look at the lives of families before beginning to develop a ministry with them. The following considerations may be helpful:

— Have the parents-to-be been active members of the parish community?

— What requirements does our parish set for baptism?

— Will these enhance or hinder parents-to-be in their practice of the Catholic religion?

— How will these requirements be perceived by families approaching baptism?

— Are both parents Catholic?

— Are the families approaching baptism ecumenical families?

— Is only one parent active in his/her church?

— Is this a single-parent family? Is the parent-to-be working outside the home?

— Is this a teenage mother and/or father?

— Are the parents-to-be an older couple having their first child?

— Are both parents-to-be working outside the home?

— Is either parent employed on a second or third shift?

— Are there other youngsters to be cared for?

— Do the parents-to-be have extended family nearby whom they can call upon for assistance and support?

— Is this a stepfamily, blended family, remarried family situation?

The church has long given verbal support to families but sometimes the very way we schedule and plan sessions for families indicates our lack of genuine concern for them. Scheduling and planning are just two areas where parish staffs need to be more sensitive to the lives of families preparing for baptism.

Over the past decade local churches have developed many different styles of ministry around baptism. Again, each parish needs to find the style that suits it best:

— Peer ministry: couple/family to couple/family ministry

— Deacons doing the preparation, celebration and follow-up

— Pastoral ministers sharing this task with families

— Pastors directly preparing families for the sacrament

— Variations of all the above

The structure of these various styles develops out of the needs of families as well as the resources of those committed to baptismal ministry in the parish. Most important, they grow out of the vision and mission of each parish.

The celebration of baptism varies from parish to parish and from diocese to diocese across the country. However, in most places the norm for the sacrament is the Sunday eucharistic liturgy where the Christian community is present and participating (see *Infant Baptism in The Parish* [LTP] for a discussion of the manner and frequency of celebrating infant baptism at Sunday Mass). It is only when the community has the opportunity to share this sacred moment with families that we can reasonably expect the community to live a commitment to families: a commitment to support and challenge them on their journey of raising their children. The community's active participation in the families' development is evident in the opportunities for continued growth that the parish offers to parents and their children. Some dimensions of baptism follow-up are:

— nursery ministry with infants and toddlers who find communal worship intolerable or whose parents prefer to pray "in peace" or just need a break from the constant care needed by young children

— parent-to-parent ministry emphasizing and developing the skills of Christian parenting

— family gatherings where parents and their young children can meet to share, learn, pray, play and be with others who have similar interests, concerns, responsibilities

— early childhood programming for toddlers and other preschoolers who learn best by experiencing with their senses the sights, sounds and feelings of church

When developing a ministry with families following the celebration of baptism, questions often surface around:

— parent or child-centered activities

— nurseries, baby-sitting or cry rooms

— early childhood learning experiences or preschools

— adult catechists or teens

— certified catechists or baby-sitters

— liturgy of the word for children or children present for the entire Mass

— volunteer or paid services

— home models or school models

— family or age groupings

— home visits or phoned communications or mail

Because ministry to and with parents for baptism is really a *network of services*, it is important that these contacts be intentionally planned to ensure continuity. Networking is a way of sharing ministry with *many people* yet having a sense of the whole ministry so that families may feel that they belong to the parish community and may really be incorporated into the total life of the local church.

It is for this reason that parishes benefit from having a *coordinator* (individual or couple) responsible for managing the continuity of programs and activities for families with young children. By intentionally meeting and planning on a regular basis, coordinators and chairpersons can be sure the whole baptism ministry functions smoothly. Visions, dreams, problems, solutions, resources, materials are shared, and the aspects of the ministry are integrated into the total life of the parish. Families sense the integrity of the services involving them and their children. They experience the care that baptism ministry can offer them.

Parishes that are multicultural need to reach out to all groups. Large and small parishes experience different needs just as do rural, urban and suburban parishes. Of course, a bilingual parish catechesis for baptism preparation will provide many beautiful and added dimensions.

In the final analysis as a baptism ministry grows in a particular parish it takes on the flavor of that community and can be an appropriate way to respond to families around the celebration of baptism. The judgment of your people should be trusted! To facilitate the planning and the actual beginning of a program the following networking outline may be helpful.

Components of Networking

Baptism Preparation Coordinator
    teams/couples who prepare parents

Nursery Care Coordinator
    people who serve in the parish nursery for infants:
        Saturday Masses
        Sunday Masses
        during meetings for parents

Baptism Celebration Coordinator
    priests/deacons who preside
    liturgy team that helps plan
    families baptizing children
    various liturgical ministries
    banner makers
    hospitality
    garment makers
    candle makers
    card makers
    greeters
    music ministers
    lectors

Toddler Care Coordinator
    people who serve in the parish play area for toddlers:
        Saturday Masses
        Sunday Masses
        during meetings for parents
        play group for children

Early Childhood Coordinator
    religious education programs for:
        three-year-olds
        four-year-olds
        five-year-olds
        parents of threes, fours and fives

Home Visitor Coordinator
    visit parents
    make phone calls
    send mailings/invitations

Beginning Family Coordinator
    people who coordinate gatherings of parents/families:
        retreat nights
        talks
        family gatherings

mothers' coffees
dads' gatherings

Baptism Anniversary Card Coordinator
people who send greetings from parish each year
for the anniversary of baptisms

Cry Rooms and Nurseries

The question is often asked as parishes build or renovate worship spaces, "What about a cry room or a nursery?" Sadly, some opt for a cry room and then expect those with infants and toddlers to spend their weekend worship time there! Consider the difference between the words "nursery" and "cry room" and some implications of each word.

Cry rooms in many churches are places where parents resent being, where they can neither see nor hear nor participate in what is going on, where crying children are hushed and where sometimes latecomers "hang out."

Nurseries are experienced as places, usually a bit removed from the community's worship space, where infants and toddlers are left in the care of adults and/or teens whose ministry it is to give care to the children while parents participate in the communal prayer of the community. The care givers are not themselves trying to worship and care for the children simultaneously as are parents in the cry room. The nursery is *designed for children*. It is a safe, creative and warm environment where babies can be rocked, fed or changed. Toys and appropriate activities are available for the toddlers and the message is clear that the space belongs to them . . . at least for the time being.

Nurseries can be staffed by parents on a cooperative basis; once every three or four weeks each parent takes a turn. This depends upon the number of families using the service. The details can be worked out easily once the decision is made to provide a "cooperative nursery."

Another option for staffing is for parents to pay the care givers each week. A responsible person is in charge of the whole nursery operation while young people, teens, older people and others who enjoy being with young children are paid to care for the infants and toddlers. Besides doing something they enjoy the care givers can make a small amount of money and parents can feel confident that their children are in good hands while they pray. The American Red Cross has a training program for certifying care givers to serve in this capacity and handle emergency situations properly. It is important for the baptism program coordinator or nursery coordinator to meet regularly with the care givers to affirm them and offer help in problem solving. Otherwise, it can become a "job for making a little spending money," and the sense of service and Christian community may be obscured.

The important aspect of nursery ministry is that it awakens in the infants and toddlers a sense of church and provides parents with a visible sign that the church responds to their needs and recognizes their gifts. It frees parents to be eucharistic ministers, lectors or music ministers. The nursery experience needs to be life-giving for the youngsters, their parents and the care givers!

As parishes develop nursery ministries, options can be explored. There are many ways to convert present "cry rooms" into usable nurseries.

Love, acceptance and care during the first three years of life are the child's earliest experiences of church: the underpinnings for continued growth and development. As a church we pray that one day children will make unique responses to their baptismal calling and make their own baptismal commitment. Until that day, we walk in hope, encouraging and challenging young children and their families.

Early Childhood

When we consider parish services to families with young children, we often think of preschool programming. I prefer the term "early childhood learning experiences," because the child's earliest experiences at home, in the neighborhood and within the church setting are part of his or her religious formation and development. "Preschool" implies that *the real learning* takes place in school. "This is just something we do with little kids until they are old enough for kindergarten or first grade." In our hearts we know that all learning is developmental, and research supports this. Let our use of words not betray us or tell only part of the story! In this reflection I will use the term early childhood to include ages three, four, five and six.

Many programs are available to parishes who choose to develop an early childhood ministry. In selecting texts and other materials for early childhood programs, it is important that they be holistic in nature: integrating prayer, music, song, art, creative movement, puppetry and storytelling, gross and fine motor skills with the teaching that is presented. Children learn through their senses, so an experiential approach is essential. They need every possible opportunity to see, hear, touch, taste and smell how good God is! Teams need to study published programs and carefully choose the one most consonant with the parish mission or vision. Some need to create their own sessions. Preview materials generally are available from diocesan offices of religious education.

Parental Involvement

Essential elements of any program for the children are catechist formation and parent involvement. Adults ministering with young children need opportunities themselves to grow in faith and in skills, to relate with and catechize youngsters in these formative years. Children, especially, need visible signs and concrete experiences to help them understand and believe. The best signs are significant people in their lives who obviously live what they say they believe.

Parents of young children are eager to hear how other parents are praying with their children, how they are sharing gospel values with them at home, how justice and peace are communicated at an early age. Providing time and space for parents to gather and discuss issues is a service that parishes can offer.

Catechist Formation

Along with active parental participation, catechist formation is essential for ministry with little ones. Those catechizing children and parents need skills as well as goodwill and deep faith. Growth in these areas most effectively happens when the adult catechists have time and opportunity to share their own journeys of faith with each other. Catechist certification programs ensure that those who minister are qualified to do so. Beyond basic catechizing skills there are other needs specific to early childhood ministry.

Early childhood ministry is very different from "baby-sitting little kids." Sometimes members of parish staffs who may not have young children of their own forget how impressionable youngsters are in these years from birth to seven. Much research has been done to substantiate what parents and early childhood catechists and teachers have known intuitively for many years: The years of most significant growth and development are the years from birth through six. During that time the foundation is laid for future learning and continued healthy development of the child. From a helpless infant to an active, inquisitive and quite independent child—the human person progresses in only six years. Truly a wonder of God! Catechists are part of that growth process and through them and his or her parents the child senses what it means to be a faithful follower of the risen Christ and an active member of the church. This role is both a blessed privilege and an awesome responsibility!

Ministry with Parents, Infants, Toddlers, Young Children

The most effective way to develop family ministry with parents and their infants, toddlers and young children is to ask parents for input at the beginning stages of the process. Their direction and creativity in planning and evaluating events must be used.

Openended questions need to be posed in the baptism discussions. New parents have great hopes and dreams; baptism is an excellent time to tap into their creativity. A few possibilities for questions might be:

— How can our parish assist you in Christian parenting?

— What can our parish do with you to assist in sharing the values that you feel are important with your child?

— What can you give to this parish?

— What gifts do you see yourself able to share at this time? In the future?

Parents of young children are gifted people, though sometimes their financial resources are limited. We need to encourage them to share the greatest gift they have: their presence with the church. What a powerful witness! To paraphrase a popular poster, "The birth of a child is God's opinion that the human race should continue." Parents' presence in our midst, particularly with their children, is a strong statement about the future of church. Baptism is a "gifted moment," an excellent time to dwell upon the need to give as well as to receive.

Celebrations

During the years following baptism, family gatherings built around various stages of the children's development are options to be considered. These can be held in each local church or can be sponsored by a cluster of parishes.

Anniversary celebrations are a possible starting point for such family gatherings. Families who have celebrated baptism during the past year are invited to come together. This gathering might take the form of a picnic, an ice cream social, a potluck supper: something informal where little kids can also participate and have a good time. As the children grow, these anniversary gatherings can become annual events. One parish had a large anniversary cake with sections for each family with the child's name and date of baptism. After the prayer and singing the children blew out their candles and each took their piece of cake to share. Simple games and activities were planned for older siblings and there was plenty of informal conversation time for the adults.

If a parish celebration of baptism anniversaries is not feasible then at least a card or note of congratulations might be sent to the child and his or her family each year. Another possibility is an appropriate and helpful article or story.

Family gatherings might also center around feasts and seasons in the liturgical year. An Advent or Christmas gathering of families with their infants, toddlers and young children could easily focus on the celebration of Christmas in the home. Lent and Easter are also potentially successful focal points. The possibilities are limited only by energy and imagination.

As the years of early childhood pass, families change along with their children. Their interests broaden and they become able to participate in more parish activities. With infants and toddlers in the home it is often difficult to have time left for much more than parenting and working. As the youngsters grow, parents feel the need to be with others in similar situations. Support groups are helpful. Parents realize their concerns are generally shared by *many* others. Together they search for answers and share experiences.

Follow-up

The ongoing nature of follow-up cannot be stressed too much. Sometimes parish leaders are good at one-time events but weak at continuing what has been started. Some churches may form play groups for the youngsters meeting regularly at the parish facility or in homes. This gives parents a chance to talk while the children play. This ministry may also take the form of a baby-sitting co-op, a mothers' coffee or "Mom's Day Out."

When families experience parish support for a few years, it is difficult for them not to get the message: "We love you. We care for you. We challenge you and we thank God for your presence among us!"

How Did We Get Here?

Until the last few centuries, religious formation of children and youth took place within the family and church community. In the early days of our nation's history, Catholic schools were founded to assist the immigrants in maintaining their cultural as well as Catholic identity in a land in which they often found themselves a minority. Later the Confraternity of Christian Doctrine (CCD) was commissioned to instruct those children who were not attending a Catholic school. The

Catholic schools and parish CCD programs continued to fill the need of educating children and youth in the faith right until the time of Vatican II.

The Second Vatican Council restored to parents and families their primary role as the religious models and formers of their children. For many parents today this is a new idea. Because parents themselves attended Catholic schools or CCD programs for their formal religious education, they often feel ill-prepared to accept their responsibility to direct the religious formation of their offspring. Parents today lack models of their elders, because for the past three or four generations the focus has shifted from a family-based to a school- or CCD-based responsibility.

Parents intend well and try hard. Many search for the knowledge and tools they need to do what they desire for their children. Often they turn to the institutional church and sadly find little support for their task, particularly at the beginning of their parenting experiences. As families face crises, the church is present but frequently lacks an active involvement in the living experiences of families.

Getting Started

Baptism is a moment of welcome and encouragement for families and the parish. Taking time to assess the needs of families with young children in the local church is the appropriate step in a formal baptismal catechesis. In looking seriously at real family experiences we may find people in our parish who feel the indifference and neglect of our church. Perhaps baptism is a way for us to reach out and offer support to meet some of the needs of these families in developing their skill and deepening their understanding so that they may actively direct the religious formation of their children. During the years following the celebration of baptism we can follow through and work with families to change the structures of our parish that so often alienate the very people we want to serve.

Parents need to learn to trust the institutional church, and the institutional church needs to be honest in respecting parents and their role as the primary faith community from which children come. The church—you and I—needs to strengthen family life from its beginnings.

In these ways families learn to look to others in the church and trust that their needs will be met; others look to them and know that together we will "live justly, love tenderly and walk humbly with our God" (Micah 6). What better time to begin than when parents approach the church for the baptism of their child!

Conclusion

Baptismal ministry is like a kaleidoscope. There are many shapes, many colors that form the design, and the design changes as the colors rearrange themselves. Ministry with families and their young children is an integral part of parish life. The ministers who share this service depend on the families who make up the local church. In an active ministry for baptism preparation, celebration and follow-up, families experience the love of other Christians who are committed to live the gospel message. And everyone in the church will experience the presence of another generation of active and committed brothers and sisters working together to build the reign of God.

◆ *Marie Seaman, SFCC*

Recovering Christian Mystagogy for Contemporary Churches

THE RESTORATION OF THE CATECHUMENATE in the Roman Catholic tradition since the promulgation of the Rite of Christian Initiation of Adults in 1972 has been a gratifying pastoral success. Given its size and complexity, one might have predicted that the catechumenate—like the liturgy of the hours—would be ignored or dismissed.

On the contrary, what has occurred is a widespread interest for rethinking our pastoral care in making new Christians. The ecclesiology underlying the catechumenate has excited theologians, pastors and baptized faithful by stretching their understanding of Christian life and their image of the church.

What's Happening Today and What's Not?

One finds parishes today throughout the United States, Canada, Africa and Australia where parishioners have taken responsibility for the initiation of new members into the community. These are not professional church personnel but lay persons who have caught the spirit of the catechumenate and have committed themselves to making the catechumenate a viable process of Christian formation. These people participate by hundreds at initiation workshops and institutes throughout North America.

The restoration of the catechumenate and the dynamics of conversion that it represents have not come too soon for contemporary churches. For a number of years there has been a growing dissatisfaction with catechism class learning and a growing need for new ways to interpret what Christian conversion means in contemporary society. There continues to be concern about the decline in numbers of active church members, leaving pastoral prophets warning us that we've got to find new ways to communicate our timeless message, because something isn't working.

Although it still may be too early to judge whether the catechumenate or its equivalent is here to stay, its initial reception and influence on many levels of church thinking and praxis has thus far been a great success. Nevertheless, there is one aspect of the catechumenate that has not been successful: mystagogy.

In the workshops and institutes on the catechumenate which I have facilitated the past few years there is always that most difficult question that continues to surface: "What can we do to make the period of mystagogy or the postbaptismal period more appealing and fruitful?" The questions are arising out of a frustration that pastoral teams experience in attempting to continue the formation process after the sacraments of initiation. It appears that once people have received baptism, confirmation and eucharist, they lose motivation for continuing anything else. In their own minds they have what they want and see no further need.

Even in communities that have been successful in drawing neophytes back after the sacraments, there seems to be some doubt about what to do with the neophytes.

Is it a reasonable expectation for us to recover a spirit of mystagogy? What does it mean? What is its value?

I believe that we have lost the sense of mystagogy that the early church, especially in the fourth and fifth centuries, seemed to take to so naturally. The spirit and practice of mystagogy lies within the historical tradition of Christianity, but not all that we find in the mystagogy of the early Fathers' will we want to take for our own. We need to construct our own experience and style of mystagogy.

In addition, however, we need to return to that early period of the church to hear for ourselves what the Fathers were preaching. It is not only the content of this patristic proclamation that we need to learn, but the style, techniques and tone of delivery.

After a brief walk through some of the mystagogical literature, I will address the cultural problems we face today and conclude with several hints about where we might begin to recover the art of mystagogy for the contemporary churches.

What Was Mystagogy Like in the Patristic Period?

It is during the fourth and fifth centuries that we find the most highly developed form of mystagogy. In this early period, mystagogy is equated with Easter, with the "mysteries" celebrated in the rites of initiation: baptism, chrismation and eucharist on the night of the great Vigil. The mystagogical homilies or lectures were delivered primarily during Easter week by the bishop or on occasion by a deacon appointed by the bishop.

These mystagogical addresses to the neophytes attempted to reveal in depth what was experienced in the actual celebration of the mysteries. The mysteries were so dependent upon experience that it was regarded as impossible to discuss them before the elect were initiated into them. The bath of regeneration brought enlightenment so that now the neophytes could see more clearly what they could not grasp before. Cyril of Jerusalem put it this way:

> For some time now, true and beloved children of the church, I have desired to discourse to you on these spiritual and celestial mysteries. But I well knew that visual testimony is more trustworthy than mere hearsay, and therefore awaited this chance of finding you more amenable to my words, so that out of your personal experience I could lead you into the brighter and more fragrant meadows of Paradise on earth.[1]

We have to presume in all of this that the vigil and the rites of initiation were substantial enough to be worth remembering. We can presume that the Vigil was a true vigil, a night watch, and not just a little longer Saturday evening Mass. We have to picture water, lots of it; CHrism that filled the whole church with its perfume; candidates shivering naked in the darkness, hungry and tired from fasting and praying and scared to death about being plunged beneath the water; a eucharistic table with bread that looks like bread, and wine, perhaps the fruit of local labor. Listen to the joy and excitement about the Vigil as Gregory of Nyssa describes his experience:

> What have we seen? A light like a cloud of fire of the candles burning during the night. All night our ears have resounded with psalms, hymns and spiritual chants. It was like a river of joy running through our ears to our soul and filling us with blessed hopes. And our heart, delighted by what we heard and saw, was marked with ineffable joy, conducting us by means of the visible spectacle to the invisible.[2]

Already we have the first test to our own attempts at mystagogy. Is our liturgy worth remembering a week later? Were the sights and sounds strong enough to herald for a week?

What stands out as characteristic in these early writings is the constant reference to the liturgy and the beautiful poetry used to communicate the depth of meaning behind all the symbols and gestures. There is a beautiful interweaving of biblical stories and the baptismal event. The writings of the Fathers, especially during this Golden Period, are filled with rich imagery and metaphor. Listen again to Cyril of Jerusalem:

> Then you were conducted by the hand to the holy pool of sacred baptism, just as Christ was conveyed from the cross to the sepulchre close at hand. Each person was asked if he or she believed in the name of the Father and of the Son and of the Holy Spirit. You made the confession that brings salvation and submerged yourselves three times in the water and emerged: By this symbolic gesture you were secretly reenacting the burial of Christ three days in the tomb. For just as our Savior spent three days and nights in the hollow bosom of the earth, so you upon first emerging were representing Christ's first day in the earth and by your immersion his first night. For at night one can no longer see but during the day one has light; so you saw nothing when immersed as if it were night, but you emerged as if to the light of day. In one and the same action you died and were born; the water of salvation became both tomb and mother for you. What Solomon said of others is opposite to you. On that occasion he said: "There is a time to be born and a time to die," but

the opposite is true in your case: There is a time to die and a time to be born. A single moment achieves both ends and your begetting was simultaneous with your death.[3]

The strong emphasis in the East on the cross and the tomb is understandable because of the proximity of the holy places themselves as centers of pilgrimage. Thus it was not only the liturgical expression of the cross and tomb to which the Eastern Fathers could point but to the revered holy places associated with the Lord's passion, death and resurrection. The pilgrim Egeria has left a wonderful diary of all she witnessed on her pilgrimage to these holy places.

As to the style of catechesis, consider the catechesis of Gregory of Nazianzus preaching at Constantinople in 381 on enlightenment:

Enlightenment is the splendor of souls, the conversion of life, the Godward conscience. It is the aid to our weakness, the renunciation of the flesh, the following of the Spirit, the fellowship of the Word, the improvement of the creature, the overwhelming of sin, the participation of light, the dissolution of darkness. It is the chariot to God, the dying with Christ, the perfecting of the mind, the bulwark of faith, the keys of the kingdom of heaven, the change of life, the removal of slavery, the loosing of chains, the remodeling of the whole person. Why should I go into further detail? Enlightenment is the greatest and most magnificent of the gifts of God. For just as we speak of the Holy of Holies, and the Song of Songs, as more comprehensive and more excellent than others, so is this called enlightenment, more holy than any other enlightenment we possess.[4]

Three Emphases in Patristic Writings

The early Fathers did not preach so eloquently simply to provide a body of Christian poetry. There was a pastoral purpose and message behind all their discourses. They wanted the neophytes to penetrate deeply into the mysteries from different angles. I find it helpful to study their writings in three basic categories, all of which undoubtedly complement one another.

First, there are the sermons and writings that are directed toward forming the neophytes in a *liturgical spirituality*. They were not meant simply as an explanation of the liturgy. More specifically, they were to help the neophyte adopt a sacramental vision of life. The mystagogical catechesis would lead them to a deeper appreciation not only of liturgical rites but to an understanding of all of life, the times and seasons and their very own way of living from a sacramental perspective.

Second, mystagogical literature was intended to be *doctrinal*, the fundamentals of faith. Frequent topics included creation, the Trinity, the incarnation, redemption and the divinization of the creature. Some of the doctrinal input was already beginning to develop from a desire for tried and true orthodoxy in light of the emerging theological controversies of the day.

Third, there was the *pastoral* material, characterized by its frequent admonitions for a sinless moral life. This included instructions on the implications of baptism for a holy life.

Here is a sampling of each category. First, in a desire to foster a sacramental vision of life, we turn to Basil the Great, who firmly proposed the uniqueness of Easter for initiation:

> Therefore any time is suitable for obtaining salvation through baptism, be it day or night, or at a precise hour or the briefest moment. But assuredly that time should be considered most appropriate which is closest in spirit to it. What could be more akin to baptism than the day of the Pasch? For that day commemorates the resurrection, and baptism makes the resurrection possible for us. Let us receive the grace of the resurrection on the day of the resurrection.[5]

A lesser-known writer in the early Church, Asterius, bishop of Amasea in Pontus, spoke eloquently about the holiness and grace-giving night which saw Christ rise from the dead:

> O Night brighter than day;
> O Night brighter than the sun;
> O Night whiter than snow;
> O Night more brilliant than torches;
> O Night more delightful than paradise;
> O Night which knows not darkness;
> O Night which has banished sleep;
> O Night which has taught us to join vigil with angels;
> O Night terror of demons;
> O Night most desirable in the year;
> O Night of torchbearing for the bridegroom in the church;

O Night mother of the newly baptized;
O Night when the devil slept and was stripped:
O Night in which the inheritor brought the beneficiaries into their
   inheritance,
An inheritance without end.[6]

In a sermon to the neophytes, John Chrysostom beautifully suggests to the newly baptized that they have become stars shining in the daytime, implying from this the sacramental role the neophytes will play in this world. While so many passages in the writings of the Fathers point to the sign and symbols in the liturgy, here Chrysostom points to the neophytes:

> Blessed be God! Behold, there are stars here on earth too, and they shine forth more brilliantly than those of heaven! There are stars on earth because of him who came from heaven and was seen on earth. Not only are these stars on earth, but—a second marvel—they are stars in the full light of day. And the daytime stars shine more brilliantly than those which shine at night. For the night stars hide themselves away before the rising sun, but when the Sun of Justice shines, these stars of day gleam forth still more brightly. Did you ever see stars which shine in the light of the sun? Yes, the night starts disappear with the end of time; these daytime stars shine forth more brightly with the coming of the consummation.[7]

Second, the doctrinal element in the mystagogical sermons of the Fathers runs through all their work. A few examples of their direct approach to passing on the doctrinal tradition may be helpful.

St. Ambrose, in his sermons on the sacraments, offers an early development of a eucharistic catechesis. Remember again that this mystagogical catechesis is being delivered only after the neophytes have experienced the actual sharing of the eucharistic table. And so while it is a strong doctrinal teaching, it has as its purpose uncovering what one experienced in the liturgy:

> Notice each detail. The day before he suffered, it says, he took bread in his holy hands. Before it is consecrated, it is bread; but when the words of Christ have been uttered over it, it is the body of Christ. Listen to what he says then: "Take and eat of this, all of you, for this is my body." And the chalice, before the words of Christ, is full of wine and water. But when the words of Christ have done their work, it becomes the blood of Christ which redeemed the people. So you can see the ways in which

the word of Christ is powerful enough to change all things. Besides, the Lord Jesus himself is our witness that we receive his body and blood. Should we doubt his authority and testimony?

Let us return to my argument. That manna rained down from heaven for the Jews was a mighty and awe-inspiring work. But think: Which is greater, manna from heaven or the body of Christ? Surely the body of Christ, who is the maker of heaven. Besides, those who ate the manna are dead. But those who eat this body have their sins forgiven and will never die.

So the answer, "Amen," you give is no idle word. For you are confessing in spirit that you receive the body of Christ. So, too, when you come up for communion, the bishop says to you: "The body of Christ." And you say "Amen," that is, "It is true." What your lips confess let your heart hold fast.[8]

Theodore of Mopsuestia in his "Third Baptismal Homily" attempted to offer an instruction on the Trinity based on the threefold immersion of baptism. It is hard to imagine that this profound teaching could be easily grasped by the neophytes, but it gives evidence of teaching profound theological truths.

Three times you immerse yourself, each time performing the same action, once in the name of the Father, once in the name of the Son and once in the name of the Holy Spirit. Since each person is named, you understand that each enjoys equal perfection and each is able to dispense the graces of baptism. You go down into the font once, but you bend beneath the water three times in accordance with the bishop's words, and you come up out of the font once. This teaches you that there is only one baptism and that the grace dispensed by the Father, the Son and the Holy Spirit is one and the same. They are inseparable one from the other, for they have one nature. So although each person can confer the grace, as is shown by your immersion at each of the names, we do not consider baptism to be complete until the Father, the Son and the Holy Spirit have all been invoked. Since their substance is one and their divinity is one, it follows that it is by a single will and a single operation that the Father, Son and Holy Spirit regularly act upon their creatures. So we too can hope for new birth, second creation and, in short, all the graces of baptism only upon the invocation of the Father, the Son and the Holy Spirit—an invocation which we believe to be the cause of all our blessings.[9]

One would have to wonder how much of the doctrine communicated to the neophytes was really meant for their ears. Others besides the neophytes would gather for these instructions. As theological differences began to develop, these mystagogical catecheses became an available forum for the notable bishop orators to teach their viewpoint. One can also begin to sense in these theological/doctrinal discourses a distinction in theological schools beginning to develop.

Third, the pastoral or moral admonitions to the neophytes are found in all of the Fathers. Augustine makes an interesting appeal for the neophytes to practice mercy in the form of forgiveness and almsgiving:

> This day is a symbol of perpetual joy for us, for the life which this day signifies will not pass away as this day is going to pass away. And so I urge and entreat you to direct your entire reason for being Christians and for carrying his name on your forehead and in your heart solely to that life which we are destined to enjoy with the angels, where there is perpetual peace, everlasting happiness, unfailing blessedness, with no anxiety, no sadness, no death.
>
> In the meantime, until we come to that rest, let us work well in this time when we are laboring and are in darkness as long as we do not see what we hope for and as long as we are making our way through the desert until we arrive at that heavenly Jerusalem as at the land of promise overflowing with milk and honey.
>
> Therefore, since temptations do not cease, let us work well. Let medicine be always at hand, as though kept near to be applied to our daily wounds. Moreover, there is a healing power in good works of mercy. For, if you wish to obtain the mercy of God, be merciful.[10]

Gregory of Nyssa is straightforward in his moral appeal. There's no question that for this pastor of the church there was to be some recognizable change evident in the neophyte. Gregory preaches:

> Before baptism, the person was wanton, covetous, grasping at the goods of others, a reviler, a liar, a slanderer, and all that is kindred with these things and consequent from them. Let the person now become orderly, sober, content with his own possessions and imparting from them to those in poverty, truthful, courteous, affable—in a word, following every laudable course of conduct.[11]

There is a much stronger moral imperative found in the prebaptismal lectures for a visible change in one's moral behavior would have to have been proven prior to baptism. It was presumed that once you were baptized you were already converted and thus should not need as much exhortation to live an honorable and virtuous life.

Connections with Contemporary Churches

Having surveyed some of the patristic mystagogical literature, let us begin to make some connections to our present practice. What is it that we learn about mystagogy from these early Christian sources?

Do not overly romanticize these early sources and think that we could simply reproduce them for today's neophytes. The preaching of the Fathers, like all good preaching, is conditioned by the context, both time and place and composition of the community. Not all of their preaching would be something we would want to emulate. The Fathers worked out of their biases and prejudices. John Chrysostom, for example, had a difficult time hiding his anti-Semitic feelings. There are, nevertheless, a few conclusions we can draw that may lead us to a contemporary praxis of mystagogy.

Mystagogy relies upon the experience of the sacred mysteries powerfully celebrated in the rites of the church and its sacred calendar. A true mystagogical catechesis cannot be readily given without reference to what one has personally experienced. To do so would be to render the catechesis abstract and disconnected from experience. Even the more highly sophisticated doctrinal catechesis relates back to the ritual or formative experience of the neophyte.

I suspect the majority of catechesis today is given prior to the experience of the celebrated mysteries as if doctrinal knowledge were the only prerequisite sign of readiness for sacramental participation. This leads us to focus only on requirements for the reception of the sacraments of initiation.

Our postsacramental catechesis does not necessarily draw out the depth of the mystery as connected with our lives. This applies not only to baptism and eucharist, but to other key ritual experiences such as marriage or the death of a loved one.

The time context of mystagogy is primarily the Easter season. Here the experience of the initiation sacraments is still fresh. Here the prayers and scriptures of the season prolong and support what began at the paschal Vigil. Even in churches that observe the liturgical calendar, Easter often means Easter day and not a rich experience of 50 days culminating with Pentecost. Thus the spirit and dynamic of Easter that is the supporting stage for mystagogy is weak or lost. The piety of average Christians tends to be lopsided with a great deal of spiritual effort made during Lent but a return to the ordinary on Easter Monday. While Easter Vigil is once again slowly reclaiming its preeminent position in the church calendar, the 50 days of Easter still need more attention.

The Rite of Christian Initiation of Adults (237) gives the Sunday eucharist during the Easter season as the principle setting for mystagogy. This is because of the relevance of the Easter lectionary as well as what we hope would be a sustained Easter focus in the preaching, the singing, the praying and the environment. The Easter season becomes the lens through which we view all of life.

The dynamic of mystagogy as is clearly demonstrated by the early church Fathers is not clever rhetoric but poetry, metaphor, story, image making and song. It is an activity that requires the use of our imagination and a reflective spirit. Mystagogy is better suited to dreamers than to scientists.

Mystagogy doesn't fit the thinking patterns of contemporary men and women. Neil Postman, in *Amusing Ourselves to Death,*[12] makes the point strongly that we have given in so unconditionally to a passive entertainment mode that we no longer think creatively. We are amusing ourselves to death. Mystagogy demands that we use our imagination and think creatively.

Teachers frequently complain that their students expect to be entertained in class. They report an amazing decline in their students' imagination and ability to think creatively. Youth may be bright but unable to use their imagination to find meaning in art and symbol and to articulate their ideas and feelings in words and other media.

We have to recognize the ways that our culture and its entertainment mode of life adversely affect our ability to use the imagination. Mystagogy does not despise reason in favor of the affective. Rather it requires a careful blend of the imagination and experience together with critical reflection. Without imagination, without a reflective mind and heart, even worthy celebrations of the liturgy may be lost.

The implication is that not only for mystagogy, but for a better experience of liturgy and more effective catechesis, we have to work at stimulating the imagination as well as developing critical thinking. And we need to begin at a very early age.

If we want to restore mystagogy in our churches, we're going to have to call forth mystagogues. Until we've experienced mystagogy, we may not know what we're trying to pass on. We must presume a rich baptismal piety in our own lives. We ourselves have to be filled with the kind of exuberance and awe the early Fathers seemed to have whenever they spoke about baptism and Easter.

The early church fathers obviously took baptism very seriously. Their unreserved joy and spiritual vigor drew me to reflect more deeply upon the meaning of my own baptism and led me to a deeper conversion and to pursue further study in the rites of Christian initiation. The value of returning to these early Christian classics is to catch a flavor for mystagogy and pray to God we can experience enough of it to intern as mystagogues ourselves.

As we learn to do mystagogy and become mystagogues, we need to be alert for what could be contemporary forms of mystagogy. One example described by Jann Fullenwieder, a pastor of the Evangelical Lutheran Church in America, draws our attention to the baptismal waters. By her recall of many biblical images, Pastor Fullenwieder opens us up to the richness of this element where we encounter the mysteries:

> For we are not here alone, standing before and in this astonishing pool of grace. Fed by the righteous stream struck in the side of Jesus, the paschal vigil waters are the source of all waters. All crashing floods, small streams and drinks begin here in Jesus' self-giving passion. We are awash, afloat and alive in Jesus in the paschal waters. All lives are conjoined here, all meanings commingled eternally.
>
> Welling up here are all other waters of time, and in them, with the baptizands of vigil night, stand all other beloved of God. There, feet still wet from Eden's rivers, are wide-eyed Adam and Eve awash finally in true wisdom. There, crossing this river and home from exile, is Jacob-Israel. There is Hagar, eyes shining to see this spring of life in the midst of the desert of death, and with her Ishmael drinking in life. Miriam dances by these waters of saving victory. Moses, smuggled through these waters by God, lives and splashes drink from the rock. Noah,

brandishing the chrism of joyful liberation broken from the tree of balm, stands in the flood with Naaman the stubborn one, eternally healed and beautiful. There too is the beggar of Siloam, giving God praise with eternally new eyes. Peter walks on these waters, no longer flailing at grace. Elijah is wakened here, to find unfailing waters in abundance. There is the crowd of Cana guests, drinking in sweet waters. There too a woman weeps in joy, her spirit cleansed in the washing of Christ's feet, John the Baptist, humble in washing our Lord, stands immersed in Christ in these paschal streams. Mary the virgin, in whose waters Jesus grew, grows with us here full of grace. The whole host, known and unknown, peers into the darkness with us, searching waters that shine with the gladness of the risen one.[13]

Mystagogy is a communal experience. Not only were the neophytes present for the homilies and lectures, but the veteran faithful were present as well. Besides the benefits the veteran faithful acquired, they undoubtedly were a source of encouragement for the neophytes. It would be into this time-tested community that the neophytes would be assimilated.

The value of the community's participation then and now would also seem to be the occasion for some realistic sharing of how the mysteries have been lived out in this people. Surely it would not have been the eloquence of the local bishop alone which unfolded the mysteries for the neophytes. Can we not presume there were personal tales and stories of elders and others which helped to clarify what was heard together from the notable pastors?

Is Mystagogy Here to Stay?

With all of these cautions, what is the forecast? Can we expect to see mystagogy in our contemporary churches? Is it really valuable enough for us to continue to work on?

Yes, mystagogy is possible. And yes, it is worth our efforts, not only for neophytes. John Chrysostom once said:

Since we have benefited from so great a gift, let us show abundant zeal and let us remember the contract we have made with him. I speak both to you, the neophytes, and to you who have long since been initiated— even many years ago. For the instruction is the same for us all, for all of us have made our agreement with him, writing it not in ink but in the spirit, not with the pen but with our tongue.[14]

For most initiated adults, the experience of baptism and first eucharist is too distant to recall, especially in churches that practice infant baptism. However, there is a value in calling to memory the fact of one's baptism, or, as Chrysostom put it, "remembering the contract." This remembering is not an attempt to recall the actual occasion of baptism and reconstruct the scene with all the participants, the minister and the christening party that followed. The memory we speak of here is not knowledge but faith-memory. Believers are invited to make a memorial, to believe in such a way as to ratify the presence of yesterday in today. And so, to remember our baptism is to activate its power in us in the present.

For the already initiated, life needs to be an ongoing discovery or mystagogy of what it means to be adopted, divinized and redeemed. If, in baptism, we have put on Christ, the entirety of our life needs to be spent imitating Christ whose name we bear as Christians. John Chrysostom clearly extended the meaning of neophytes to include us all when he said, "Imitate him, you also, I implore you, and you will be called neophytes not only for two, three, ten or twenty days, but you will still merit this name after ten, twenty or thirty years, and in fact for all of your lives."

The challenge entrusted to pastors is to keep the baptismal memory alive so that we live our life from a baptismal dimension. Every Eastertime becomes again the stage for stirring up the memory of our baptism through a contemporary mystagogical catechesis. The baptism of new members, the renewal of baptismal vows, the paschal Vigil, the Easter candle, the Easter eucharist, the hymns and psalms and lectionary for Eastertime all become the catalyst for an ongoing mystagogical catechesis. All of these freshly-experienced sacramentals and rites keep the memory of our baptism before us.

Mystagogy is defined as "a time for the community and the neophytes together to grow in deepening their grasp of the paschal mystery and in making it part of their lives" (RCIA, 234). The only way we can begin to deepen our grasp of the paschal mystery is by remembering our own baptism, by enlivening our memory of that radical bath of regeneration.

And so, now I call upon you, since I love you more, O Neophyte, dear to me. Always be what you have been called, one newly baptized everywhere, pleasing on every occasion, beautiful always, not a bridegroom today and unwed tomorrow, for this has married you to the Lord, our resurrection.[15]

♦ *Ron Lewinski*

Notes

1. Cyril of Jerusalem, "The Prebaptismal Rites," *Mystagogical Catechesis* 1, E. Yarnold, SJ, editor, *The Awe-Inspiring Rites of Initiation* (London: St. Paul Publishing Company, 1971), 68.

2. Gregory of Nyssa, "On the Sacred Feast of the Pasch and on the Resurrection," A. Hamman, OFM, editor, *The Paschal Mystery*, Sermon 3, *Ancient Liturgies and Patristic Texts* (NY: Alba House, 1969), 96.

3. Cyril of Jerusalem, "The Baptismal Rite," *Mystagogical Catechesis,* Sermon 2, Yarnold, *Rites,* 76.

4. Gregory of Nazianzus, "Sermon on Holy Baptism," Hamman, OFM, editor, *Baptism,* Sermon 4, *Ancient Liturgies and Patristic Texts* (NY: Alba House, 1967), 89.

5. Basil the Great, "Protreptic on Holy Baptism," *Protrepticus* 2, Hamman, *Baptism,* 76.

6. Asterius, "Joseph and Jesus," Homily 19 on Psalm 5, Hamman, *The Paschal Mystery*, 108.

7. John Chrysostom, "Sermon to the Neophytes," Sermon 1, Hamman, *Baptism*, 165.

8. Ambrose of Milan, "Sermons on the Sacraments," 4, *The Sacraments,* Yarnold, *Rites,* 137–38.

9. Theodore of Mopsuestia, "Baptismal Homily 3," *Homilies* 20, ibid., 202.

10. Augustine of Hippo, "Baptism," *Sermons,* 259, Hamman, *Baptism,* 216.

11. Gregory of Nyssa, "On the Baptism of Christ: A Sermon for the Feast of the Lights," Hamman, *Baptism,* 135.

12. Postman, Neil, *Amusing Ourselves to Death* (NY: Penguin Books, 1985).

13. Jann Fullenwieder, "Newborn in Paschal Waters," *Liturgy* 7, 1 (Summer, 1987), 55–59.

14. John Chrysostom, "Sermon to the Neophytes," 1, *Sermons,* 6, Hamman, *Baptism,* 170.

15. *Kontakia of Romanos, Byzantine Melodist*, II: *On Christian Life*, translated by Marjorie Carpenter (Columbia MO: University of Missouri Press, 1973).

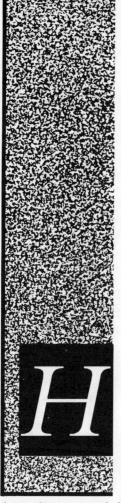

How Do Initiatory Symbols Come Alive for Adults?

How can we make the initiatory symbols come alive for those being baptized as adults? Things like water, fragrant oil, shared food and drink so easily stir up feelings of newness, wonder and belonging in children. Long familiarity with these elements and the practical human and ecological problems that attend them often leave adults without the child's natural affinity for the symbolic meaning of things. And so our question. Can we infuse our sacramental catechesis for adult catechumens with that same freshness? How can we help them break open the experience summed up in those great symbols of being bathed, anointed and invited to sit down at table for the first time with the community?

From the outset we should note the limited perspective of this essay. The preceding chapters have already dealt with both pre- and postbaptismal catechesis of adult catechumens in a broader way. Here we narrow our focus to one part of that ministry, namely, to sacramental catechesis and especially to the initiatory symbols. This chapter first sets the stage with several reminders about key dimensions of liturgy and sacramental catechesis, then it explores some of the great initiatory symbols, and finally it expresses some hopes for a sacramental cate-chesis of adult catechumens that truly comes alive.

A learning process is shaped and guided by two crucial elements: what we are to learn about and who the learners are. Accordingly, the following brief reminders about liturgy and adult sacramental cate-chesis may be in order.

About Liturgy

First, the liturgy about which the catechumens are to learn is not text and rubric. Rather, it is an action, an event of worship and salvation. At the heart and center of liturgy lie the dying and rising of Christ, the paschal event which glorifies God and sets us free.[1]

Second, the risen Lord, who alone is "the minister [*leitourgos*] of the sanctuary and of that true tabernacle set up . . . by the Lord" (Hebrews 8:12), stands at the center of our assembly as minister and liturgist. It is he who speaks the word we proclaim, who acts in the sacrament we celebrate (*Constitution on the Sacred Liturgy* [CSL], 7). "It is through him that we address our Amen to God when we worship together." (1 Corinthians 1:20) But as that phrasing suggests, he is not the sole liturgical protagonist. Christ associates the church with himself, as Vatican II says, making the liturgy both his action and that of his body, the church (CSL, 7). From this flows the critical importance of the presence and the full, conscious, active participation of the assembly underscored several times by the council (CSL, 14, 27). Even though there are special roles of ministry within the liturgical assembly (CSL, 26), in a fundamental way the liturgy remains the action of the assembly, gathered with its risen Lord to keep covenant.

Third, liturgical speech and action are highly symbolic in charac-ter. Anthropologists and liturgists remind us that symbols have multi-ple meanings which defy reduction to one simple explanation; rituals enact meaning rather than simply tell us about it. So, too, with liturgy.

Symbols have their habitat in dialogue and group interchange. They are born for encounter and communication. Liturgical symbols sweep up a gathered people into an interchange within the assembly and with their God, enacting a covenantal relationship between them. Finally, though we first think of material things such as rings and candles and water when we speak of symbols, they are symbols only because of the symbolic ways in which we use them. We exchange the rings, light the candles and sprinkle one another with water. Action is the root symbol. Those objects, chosen because something about them anticipates what the action itself will say, embody the meaning of the action. The actions in turn become the bearers and cherished keepsakes that bring meaning to life in memory and in ritual reenactment. The fundamental liturgical symbols, then, are not things, but rather the actions of the assembly that make use of those things.

Fourth, there is both a human and a Christian root for the symbolism of sacraments. The actions we perform in the assembly are human actions with a long history of symbolic human meaning. But they are also actions that have been caught up in a history of religious usage in which the human symbolism has been transformed with saving meaning.

Such is the liturgy about which we are to do the catechesis—a moment when the church gathers with its risen Lord to proclaim his good news and enact the paschal mystery, embodying the saving meaning of that moment in a rich variety of symbolic actions and objects.

About Sacramental Catechesis

The fact that we are dealing with adult catechumens reminds us first that adult learning methods are required. As the *National Catechetical Directory*[2] (NCD) points out, adults are to play a central role in their own catechesis. The catechesis should respect and make use of their own experience. It should help them reflect on that experience in the light of faith and translate their reflection into practical action (NCD, 185d).

Second, the sacramental catechesis of adult catechumens takes place within the *Rite of Christian Initiation of Adults*, a document that stresses process and community. The catechumen is called to make a spiritual journey of faith and conversion in the midst of the community (RCIA, 4–5), moving first through a period of pastoral formation shaped by catechesis, shared community life, liturgical participation and mission (catechumenate). Then, the senior catechumen moves through a time of intense preparation for the initiatory sacraments (purification or enlightenment) and finally into a time of mystagogy or postbaptismal catechesis. Sacramental catechesis follows the same pattern, unfolding in pre- and postbaptismal phases designed not just to teach adults about sacraments but to help them grow in the Christian way of life which those sacraments celebrate.

Third, the fact that the catechumens are "apprentices" in the Christian way of living[3] suggests that "learning by doing" not only accompanies but also grounds "learning by reflecting" in their sacramental catechesis. If good celebration of the liturgy is itself formative and educative (NCD, 36), then that is where sacramental catechesis actually begins. If we see liturgy itself as "first theology," we might also call liturgy a "first catechesis," or "catechesis-being-born."[4] What we normally think of as sacramental catechesis is really a "second catechesis." Like "second theology," it is a form of reflection. It reflects on the liturgical experience to prepare for, open up and deepen that experience.

These reminders converge with the earlier ones that center adult sacramental catechesis, whether in anticipation or in retrospect, on the great initiatory symbols in which we experience the dying and rising of Christ. It is to those symbols that we now turn.

The Great Initiatory Symbols

We do not have to look far to find the great initiatory symbols. They are all gathered up in the mother feast of the church, the Easter Vigil. What follows is a brief reflective exercise to illustrate how we might begin to explore the vivid and rich meanings those symbols can have for ourselves and the adult catechumens.[5] In our reflection we will do well to attend to actions as well as symbolic objects and to the human-religious as well as the Christian meaning.

Gathering

The gathering of the assembly may seem a strange place to begin. However, as the United States bishops have written, "Among the symbols with which the liturgy deals, none is more important than this assembly of believers."[6] And that is where the Easter Vigil begins, with the gathering of the community and its catechumens to light a new fire in the dark of night.

The very act of gathering, whether in liturgy or in any of our myriad human groupings, accomplishes something deeply significant.[7] Gathering has an air of festivity, a feeling of anticipation as we wait for things to begin. It speaks of a common purpose, of mutual bonds, of a shared world. And so in a most fundamental way, we identify and define ourselves by gathering together, telling ourselves and the world who we are: a family gathering, a justice committee, a group of friends at a barbecue, a worshiping people. As the experience of catechumens attests, being with and being surrounded by others easily leads to a sense of belonging and an experience of being embraced by God as well.

What gathering has begun is deepened as the purposes for which the group comes together unfold. Telling the family stories, devising a strategy for promoting justice, catching up with what's happening in the lives of friends, praying to God—all these cement the sense of identity and solidarity. The United States bishops continue, "The most powerful experience of the sacred is found in the celebration and the persons celebrating, that is, it is found in the action of the assembly: the living words, the living gestures, the living sacrifice, the living meal" (*Environment and Art in Catholic Worship* [EACW], 29). Joining in the assembly's action reinforces in a catechumen that same sense of belonging.

But before we look at those actions, a corollary must be added about the assembly. It is the most natural thing in the world for a group to imprint its identity on its gathering place. Objects needed to sustain the common purpose, keepsakes and trophies from special moments, records of past transactions—these are the ·bearers of the group's memory and self-definition. The liturgical assembly also makes its imprint on the gathering space, defining itself by lectern, font and table, and remembering its story with raised cross, saintly images and holy objects enshrined. But in the end the place is held holy because a hallowed people gathers there to do what is holy.

Lighting a Candle

The first dramatic act of the people gathered to keep the vigil is to dispel the darkness of the spring night by starting a fire and lighting a candle. From cradle on, paced by the rhythms of day and night, we have known a daily passage to and fro between light and darkness. Think of the rich deposit of dimly remembered feelings and associated metaphors which that experience has left us: work/rest, comfort/fear, seeing/hiding, being seen/being hidden, knowing the way/being lost, wisdom/ignorance, life/death. Light and darkness bear all these unspoken meanings whenever we make the passage between them.

So simple an action as lighting a paschal candle inherits all these meanings. But it is also the heir to a wealth of Christian memory built on related Jewish symbolism. A simple gathering up of biblical texts tells something of that richness. "God who dwells in light inaccessible" (1 Timothy 6:16) "is clothed in light" (Psalm 104:2). "God is light and in God there is no darkness." (1 John 1:5) God's first creative act was to give light to the world (Genesis 1:3). In the fullness of time the word came into the world to be the light of the world (John 9:5). And when Christ rose from the dead, it was to proclaim light to all peoples (Acts 26:23). Baptized into Christ, we have been called from darkness into God's marvelous light (1 Peter 2:9) to walk in the light as children of the light and not in the darkness (1 John 1:6–7). Once we were darkness, but now we are light in the Lord (Ephesians 5:8), called like him to be the light of the world (Matthew 5:14). "For God, who said, 'Let light shine out of darkness,' has shone in our hearts, that we in turn might make known the glory of God shining on the face of Christ." (2 Corinthians 4:6)

These are the memories we keep as we gather around that lighted candle to sing and exult. The candle itself, decorated in honor of the one who is the light of the world, becomes the bearer of that collected meaning not only for the duration of the great Vigil, but for the entire Easter season and all subsequent baptismal gatherings of the community.

Telling the Story

Bathed now in the light of Christ, the assembly settles back to hear the shared story retold in a series of readings. We hear epic stories of God's creative spirit hovering over the waters, of the ordeal in which Abraham's faith is tested, of the exodus from Egypt and the passage through the sea. We hear a prophet's words stirring in our memories echoes of ancient hopes about covenant and fidelity, about a God who provides food and drink for the asking, about a people sprinkled clean and transformed in heart. We hear the good news about Christ passing through death to life, inviting us to Easter faith and opening the way for our baptismal crossing with him.

Rehearsing the common story that enshrines the group's identity and values is something we do instinctively at times such as this. When a group takes in new members, it cannot remain the same. All, initiates and members alike, are called upon to undergo transformation and take on new roles and relationships. That is why it is important to frame and interpret what we are doing by retelling the story of who we are and where our journey leads us. In the Easter Vigil that is doubly important. For the story we tell is not simply our human story; rather it is the story of God-with-us, the word God speaks to call us into a life journey as God would have it told. This is the epic we tell not only to the catechumens in our midst but to the entire assembly as well.

An epic of such proportions fittingly welcomes a host of related symbols: an appointed place for the telling where we can return again and again to let all the noisy stories of our lives be stilled as they are transposed into a new voice, a lectern as advantageous as a town crier's roof or a messenger's mountaintop, a book as cherished and revered as the story it holds.

Bathing in Water

The story, once retold, must be acted out. And so the assembly keeping vigil leads its catechumens to the waters to bathe them into new life. And what a rich symbolism those baptismal waters have for us![8] Recall first all the meanings water has for us: thirst-quenching, cooling, washing clean, bathing, watering, fire fighting, flowing, babbling, roaring, eroding, flooding, drowning, birthing. Behind them all is a paradox: Water restores and destroys, water is life-bearing and death-dealing.

These same paradoxical meanings are caught up in the great biblical images of water: the fertile waters of creation (Genesis 1:20–23) and the destroying waters of the deluge (Genesis 7:6–23), the waters of the Red Sea granting passage to some and denying it to others (Exodus 14:10–31), the Jordan waters separating desert journey and safe homeland (Joshua 3:1–17), water trickling from a rock in the desert (Exodus 17:1–7) and dreams of rivers flowing from the stone temple of Jerusalem (Ezekiel 47:1–12), God's spirit brooding over the waters of creation (Genesis 1:1–2) and promised in an outpouring like water in the desert (Isaiah 44:3).

The symbolism continues in the life of Jesus: a Jordan baptism and Spirit poured out (Luke 3:21–22), living water for a thirsting woman (John 4:4–42), font of living water for the thirsty (John 7:37), waters of a Siloam pool to wash away a person's blindness (John 9:1–41), water poured to wash a disciple's feet (John 13:1–17), water flowing from a pierced side (John 19:34).

Water's potent symbolism is not based on the material element alone. From the very beginning when God's spirit moved the waters, water has been the arena for God's action and that of the humans God created. The meaning water can have, whether human or saving, is drawn out when someone uses the water to wash and cleanse, to slake thirst, to water, to refresh a foot-weary traveler, to sustain or threaten life.

And so to enact the story we tell in the Vigil we lead the catechumen to the baptismal font to be bathed and cleansed in its living waters, to be plunged into the death of Christ and raised up into newness of life. Even as we bathe the catechumen, God is there to act. The dancing waters reflect the waters of creation, flood, Red Sea and Jordan River with all their intimations of death and life that came to pass most fully in Jesus. Plunged into the waters and drawn up again, the catechumen passes through death to life in the one who made the passage for us all. Those waters are for the catechumens as they have been for us all: tomb and womb.

Fittingly, then, the renewed liturgy demands more than a small water basin that invites only a token cleansing. What is needed is a font flowing with living water, grand enough to sustain a larger life-and-death symbolism, in a spacious place set apart where the company of those already baptized can surround those to be bathed during the Vigil. That place of rebirth, summed up in the font and its living waters, continues to serve the assembly as memorial and entryway every time we gather for eucharist.

Anointing with Oil

For those baptized during the Vigil there is another ritual entryway to their first eucharist: through an anointing with oil. Like the oil itself, this ritual is somewhat elusive in its symbolism. In a culture where this one word refers to a wide range of things from cooking food and auto lubricants to body lotions and baby oil, the natural symbolism of oil in caring for and adorning the body may not always come to mind. But it is precisely this application of salves, oils and lotions to the body to give it strength, health and beauty that still provides the experiential base for our ritual. That basic meaning is further enhanced when the scented oil is applied by the hand of another as an expression of care and responsibility.

It is this experience that lies at the root of the rich biblical images vaguely remembered in the ritual anointing. In that culture oil spoke of bounty and blessing, of feast and gladness. It was poured lavishly on the heads of prophets, priests and kings as a mark of honor and a sign of consecration to public service. Most importantly, the outpouring of oil, like the outpouring of water, images the lavish outpouring of God's Spirit that would accompany the messianic times when the Spirit would breathe new life into the people (Ezekiel 37) and inspire a mission of lasting justice for the oppressed (Isaiah 61:1–3).

The hopes, Christians believe, came to fulfillment in Jesus the Christ, the Anointed One. In the waters of the Jordan he received an abiding outpouring of the Spirit (Luke 3:21–22). From his response to the words of Isaiah which he proclaimed in his hometown synagogue (Luke 4:17–21) and from his subsequent actions it is clear that he accepted the justice and peace ministry demanded by that gift. And when that ministry led him to death's doorstep, a woman anointed him in anticipation of his death struggle (Matthew 26:6–13; John 12:1–8), and other women intended to do the same for him in the stillness of the grave (Mark 16:1; John 19:40). In life and beyond death he is the Anointed One. All who join him there are called Christians, anointed ones.

And so in the ancient biblical way, those who rise from baptismal waters to be led to table are first anointed with fragrant oil to seal the gift of the Spirit who gives life and calls to mission. When the transition from bath to table is accomplished, the fragrance of the oil gradually fades, leaving only the lives of the baptized to remind us that it is the anointed ones who truly are the "fragrance of Christ" (2 Corinthians 2:15) in the world.

Sharing Bread and Wine

In the final part of the Easter Vigil the assembly welcomes to the table those who have been bathed and anointed with scented oil. The action flows naturally. New life in our midst is cause for rejoicing and is to be nurtured for the shared journey and the common task. But the symbolism is so rich that words can hardly begin to tell it.[9]

The underlying human actions are simple: breaking, passing around, consuming of a common loaf and a common cup. These actions already speak of family ties and bonds of friendship, of shared life and common tasks, of mutual caring and nurturing, of food and life sacrificed that another may be fed and live. And these actions are performed according to the Jewish ritual pattern used by Jesus. As Jesus did, we break and share the bread and cup with praise and thanks in prayerful remembrance of what God has done to give us salvation. We ask God to continue these gracious ways toward us.

The actions are done also in memory of Jesus. We weave the story of his last supper, and by that token the larger story of his life and death and resurrection, into the heart of our thankful recital of God's mighty deeds. Thus the meaning of our meal is subtly transformed. Jesus is table companion, giving himself to the assembly and its new members as the bread of life. And because the bread is one, all who partake of it are one body (1 Corinthians 10:17).

The food and drink are caught up in the web of transformed meaning, as are the table, the cup and plate and the place where we gather for the Lord's Supper. The bread and wine are the fruit of the earth and the vine—part of the gift of the creation that is our home and sustains our life. They are a human work—produced by the toil of many hands and the sweat of many brows. As human products, they are the repository of our ability to draw from the earth, for ourselves and one another, both daily sustenance and festive fare. But they also become a spiritual food and drink, sacramental signs of Christ's self-gift.

Romanticism about the meaning of the meal ought not, however, lead us to neglect the dark side of this food-language. The production, distribution and consumption of food and drink are indeed a language that encodes our relationship to those who produced them, to those who sit down with us to share them and to those who do not. Besides being a language of communion and interdependence, food can be turned into a language of exclusion and a weapon of oppression. At that point the dangerous memory of Jesus calls us up short. We need to remember that he was known as one who ate with outcasts and sinners (Luke 15:1) and that he taught that all were invited to the banquet (Matthew 22:2–10). Jesus transformed the act of eating and drinking together into a charged language about food that is more inclusive.[10] It is for that reason that ministry for justice and peace can never be optional for those who sit at the Lord's table. To feed on one who is "bread for the life of the world" (John 6:51) is to commit oneself to becoming like bread.

Sending

And so the Easter Vigil ends by reversing its beginning. But the sending is more than a mere ending that brings the celebration to a close. The symbolism of the sending runs far deeper. The more-seasoned Christians and the neophytes who have gathered for a time around candle, book, font and table to remember and enter into the story of Jesus must be sent back out into the world now to enact that story in lives of service.

The sending, therefore, is an act of bestowing and accepting a commission. The sending is the assembly's amen to what they have celebrated. It is their amen to the mission that lies ahead. Sending is the reason for gathering and it deserves equal care.

Some Hopes for a Sacramental Catechesis of Adult Catechumens

Such are the great initiatory symbols. How might we go about doing a sacramental catechesis that will offer the adult catechumens a fresh insight into the experience of being bathed, anointed with oil and invited to the community table?

For inspiration we need look no further than the journey to Easter faith made by the two disciples on the way to Emmaus (Luke 24:13–35). Their journey unfolds in three phases, each having implications for catechesis. The journey begins with a form of catechesis that might best be characterized as storytelling. We find the two disciples walking away from Jerusalem, rehearsing the story of Jesus' last days and death (24:13–14). A stranger approaches and walks with them, eliciting the story once again and helping them voice bitter disillusionment (15–24). He then retells that same story, seen now through the eyes of the prophets (25–27).

The second phase of their journey to Easter faith reaches a swift climax when they press him to be their dinner guest and he assumes the role of host, leading them in the breaking of the bread (28–30). As he does so, their eyes are opened and they "recognize" him (31). In that ritual moment of "first catechesis" they have come not just to know about him, but to know him.

In the third phase, a kind of mystagogy, they immediately name what they experienced on the road: "Were not our hearts burning inside us as he talked to us on the road and explained the scriptures to us?"[11] And having returned to their companions in Jerusalem, the two recount the experience in full detail and witness to the birth of their Easter faith in the breaking of the bread (33–35). With that, the pattern of their journey is complete. The initial experience along the road prepared them for the moment of disclosure that they experienced at table, and the table experience then unfolded in a new awareness and commitment to mission.

That story leads me to a threefold suggestion about how sacramental catechesis of adult catechumens might unfold.[12] I offer it not as a worked-out approach but as a hopeful series of "what if's . . ."

Evoke the Story

What if our catechetical goal for prebaptismal catechesis were to walk alongside adult catechumens with just one thing in mind: to set their hearts burning, to have them come with freshness to the sacraments?

What would that kind of catechesis look like?

The catechesis would aptly center on mutual storytelling. At every step of the way we would evoke and listen to their stories. In response, we would tell our master story summed up in the scriptures. We would take seriously the recommendation that the catechesis be "accommodated to the liturgical year" (RCIA, 75), ideally centering it on the scripture readings of Sundays, feasts and seasons. The great baptismal passages read at the celebrations of the scrutinies and during the Easter Vigil would be told and explored with great care. And the method used would not be one of exegesis, but one of "evocations of the revealed word" in which the correspondences between our stories and the biblical story are allowed to emerge.[13] That catechesis would be firmly set in the larger context of a community way of living, serving and praying (RCIA, 75).

Sacramental catechesis focuses primarily on developing the catechumen's experience of the ritual and prayer life of the community. Special care is needed to enrich the biblically based catechesis with celebrations of the word (RCIA, 75). The presentation of the Bible, now tucked away in the Rite of Acceptance into the Order of Catechumens (RCIA, 64), might well become more prominent, perhaps as a separate ritual celebration. Care also needs to be taken to help the catechumen acquire and deepen an experiential sense for the initiatory rituals. For example, more might be made of evensong with solemn candlelighting, the optional anointings (RCIA, 98–102), the Holy Thursday washing of the feet,[14] and periodic *agape* meals accompanied by a simple *berakah* prayer. In all these ritual experiences a representative portion of the local assembly would be present and participating. Given the effectiveness of these experiences and the biblical catechesis, explicit instruction on the theology and rituals of initiation might at this point be kept to a minimum, to avoid overloading the catechumens with a theoretical understanding of an experience not yet fully theirs.

Preparation for the celebration of the initiatory sacraments peaks during the time of purification and enlightenment. What better way to set hearts burning than to lead them through a growing crescendo of fresh experiences: of election, of the catechumenal journey, of the atmosphere of lenten retreat pervading the community, of the scrutinies with their epic baptismal stories, of solemn Triduum liturgies and of intensified prayer and fasting during the days before the Easter Vigil?

Let the Symbols Speak

What if in celebrating the Easter Vigil we were to keep one goal in mind: to so celebrate the initiatory sacraments that the catechumens coming to them with hearts burning could truly come to know the Lord Jesus in the breaking of the bread? Would we not have to let the central initiatory symbols speak to them? How might that take place?

Some key pastoral principles already at hand would be more carefully observed. Among all the liturgical symbols, "none is more important than the assembly. . . . The most powerful experience of the sacred is found in the celebration and the persons celebrating, that is, it is found in the action of the assembly. . . ." (EACW, 28–29). Paradoxically, that action of the assembled people is capable of inviting us into an experience of the mystery of God only when it is fully human and truly our own, not minimalized in any way (EACW, 14), and yet so performed as to invite us to "see beyond the face of the person or the thing, a sense of the holy, the numinous, mystery" (EACW, 12). What is required is "the opening up of our symbols, especially the fundamental ones of bread and wine, water, oil, the laying on of hands, until we can experience all of them as authentic and appreciate their symbolic value" (EACW, 15). A gathered people, fully human, fully at prayer, fully attentive to the divine presence in all they say and do in the assembly, truly let their symbols speak. Only then will catechumens experience the celebration as the "first catechesis."

In particular, care would be taken that the lighting of the Easter candle is not outshone by a bonfire. The story that culminates in Christ's victory over death would be told in the assembly in as compelling a way as possible. The waters in the font would be so presented and the washing so performed that both the baptized and the catechumens would be silently invited into Christ's passage between death and life.[15] Oil may be poured out so lavishly in the anointing that it leaves the assembly and those anointed enveloped in the fragrance that vividly speaks of the Anointed One and the outpouring of his Spirit. The whole company gathers at the table where the gifts of bread and wine are blessed and shared in simple yet holy gestures so that all come to know him in that breaking of the bread and eagerly go out in witness and service.

A flight of fancy? What if we truly let the symbols speak?

Break Open the Experience

And finally, what if our goal for the postbaptismal catechesis were to enable the catechumens to name their experience of the Easter sacraments, to give an account of their experience in witness and service? That kind of catechesis has to be a true mystagogy, a breaking open of the experience. What would it look like?

Postbaptismal catechesis would take its cue from what is the distinctive character and force of this period, the new, personal experience of the sacraments and of the community (RCIA, 247). The chief setting for the mystagogy would be the Sunday eucharists of Eastertime, with the readings from Cycle A (RCIA, 247). If that is so, two other things follow: The celebration itself must be such that the newly baptized continue to experience it as the "first catechesis," and the homily must provide the first and most important breaking open of that experience, not for the purpose of theoretical understanding, but for the sake of naming our faith and committing ourselves to witness and service in Christ's name, as the accounts from the Acts, proclaimed in the first readings of Cycle A, so clearly suggest. Other settings for a more leisurely and theological breaking open of the experience may be provided.

As in the prebaptismal period, postbaptismal catechesis is situated within a context of community living, reflection and mission, so that the very newness of the neophytes' experience can bring fresh vision and energy to the other members of the community (RCIA, 244–245).

Conclusion

In this chapter we have explored the great initiatory symbols with one question in mind: How can sacramental catechesis make these symbols come alive for adults, as it does for children? Despite the pragmatic haste and deteriorated quality that so constantly mark our use of these great symbols, it may be less difficult than we imagine to mount such a catechesis. The answer, in the end, seems very simple: Let the symbols speak for themselves and trust in their power. As people at prayer know in their bones, liturgical symbols are infinitely more interesting and powerful than all of our words and explanations. Do we dare let those symbols speak?

◆ *Gilbert Ostdiek,* OFM

Notes

1. Vatican II, *Constitution on the Sacred Liturgy* (CSL), 5.

2. *Sharing the Light of Faith: National Catechetical Directory for Catholics of the United States* (Washington: United States Catholic Conference, 1979).

3. See Vatican II, *Decree on the Church's Missionary Activity*, 14.

4. Paraphrasing A. Kavanagh, *On Liturgical Theology* (NY: Pueblo Publishing Co., 1984), 74.

5. Some useful general resources: M.P. Ellebracht, *The Easter Passage: The RCIA Experience* (Minneapolis: Winston Press, 1983) 111–57; G. Huck, *The Three Days: Parish Prayer in the Paschal Triduum* (Chicago: Liturgy Training Publications, 1981), 59–86; G. Huck and M.A. Simcoe, editors, *A Triduum Sourcebook* (Chicago: Liturgy Training Publications, 1983); R. Kiefer, *Blessed and Broken: An Exploration of the Contemporary Experience of God in Eucharistic Celebration*, (Wilmington: Glazier, 1982), 94–115; M.M. Kelleher, "The Meaning of Christian Spirituality," in L. Klenicki and G. Huck, editors, *Spirituality and Prayer: Jewish and Christian Understandings* (New York: Paulist Press, 1983), 19–44; M. Mick, *The Future Present: The Phenomenon of Christian Worship* (NY: Seabury Press, 1980; and the symposium: "Central Symbols," *Liturgy: Journal of the Liturgical Conference* (Summer, 1987), 5–93.

6. *Environment and Art in Catholic Worship* (EACW) (Washington DC: United States Catholic Conference, 1978), 28.

7. See L. Hoffman, "Assembling in Worship," *Worship* 56 (1982), 98–112.

8. Some resources for reflection on baptismal symbolism: J. Danielou, *The Bible and the Liturgy* (Notre Dame: University of Notre Dame Press, 1966), 70–113; D. Stanley, "The New Testament Doctrine of Baptism: An Essay in Biblical Theology," *Theological Studies* 18 (1957), 169–215; D. Stevick, "The Water of Life: Unpacking the Meanings," *Purification and Enlightenment,* Christian Initiation Resources Reader 3 (New York: Sadlier, 1984), 69–80.

9. Resources for further reflection: E. Barbotin, "The Meal," *The Humanity of Man* (Maryknoll: Orbis Press, 1975), 319–38; P. Rouillard, "From Human Meal to Christian Eucharist," *Worship* 52 (1978), 425–39; C. Vogel, "Symbols in Christian Worship: Food and Drink," L. Maldonado and D. Power, editors, *Symbol and Art in Worship,* Concilium 132 (NY: Seabury Press, 1980), 66–73.

10. Resources for further reflection: G. Feeley-Harnik, *The Lord's Table: Eucharist and Passover in Early Christianity* (Philadelphia: University of Pennsylvania Press, 1981); J. Grassi, *Broken Bread and Broken Bodies: The Lord's Supper and World Hunger* (Maryknoll:

Orbis Press, l985); M. Hellwig, *The Eucharist and the Hunger of the World* (NY: Paulist Press, 1978).

11. Readers familiar with the poetry of John Shea will recognize his image of Jesus as "the arsonist of the heart."

12. Some helpful resources for further reflection on principles of sacramental catechesis for adults: R.L. Browning and R.A. Reed, *The Sacraments in Religious Education and Liturgy* (Birmingham: Religious Education Press, 1985), especially 239–53; W. Johnston, "Gearing Up for Adult Confirmation," *The Living Light* 24 (1988), 134–42; A. Kavanagh, "Theological Principles for Sacramental Catechesis," *The Living Light* 23 (1987), 316–24; NCD, 185, 187, 189; M. Searle, "Issues in Christian Initiation: Uses and Abuses of the RCIA," *The Living Light* 22 (1986), 199–214, especially his comments on the "cultural linguistic model"; J. H. Westerhoff, *Building God's People in a Materialistic Society* (NY: Seabury Press, 1983), especially 37–78; J. H. Westerhoff and W. H. Willimon, *Liturgy and Learning through the Life Cycle* (NY: Seabury Press, 1980), 9–52.

13. Though the application is mine, I am grateful to a faculty colleague, Eloise Rosenblatt, RSM, for calling to my attention the following passage by Marie Teresa Porcile, "Water in the Slums," J. Pobee and Potter B. von Wartenberg, editors, *New Eyes for Reading: Biblical and Theological Reflections by Women from the Third World* (Geneva: World Council of Churches, 1986), 35: "There are many different ways of doing Bible study. The traditional method is to take a text or a passage, situate it in relation to its overall context (cultural, literary, etc.) and then study the text itself for its deeper meaning, analyze it, explain the sense of certain expressions, words, particular phrases, and lastly, consider how it can be applied to our own lives and how it might change them. However, there are other kinds of Bible studies which are perhaps not properly speaking 'studies' but rather evocations of the revealed word. These happen when we recognize an echo of some passage of scripture in an occurrence or event of everyday life. This is not to say that every detail of the contemporary event can be made to 'correspond' step by step with the event narrated in the Bible, but nonetheless the one evokes the other as though calling on it for help in discerning the deeper meaning of the event or current life."

14. The catechetical possibilities here are twofold. In addition to the obvious parallels that might be made between baptismal cleansing and the foot-washing (see John 13:10), recent scholarship has suggested that the foot-washing functions as a kind of "eucharistic memorial" within John's fully developed "testamentary tradition" of the eucharist. For a short presentation of the testamentary tradition, see E. LaVerdiere, "The Testament of Jesus," P. Bernier, editor, *Bread from Heaven* (NY: Paulist Press, 1977), 8–18. For a more technical treatment see X. Léon-Dufour, *Sharing the Eucharistic Bread: The Witness of the New Testament* (NY: Paulist Press, 1987).

15. For a description of how powerfully the water symbolism can be experienced, see J. Gelineau, "The Symbols of Christian Initiation," *Becoming a Catholic Christian: A Symposium on Christian Initiation* (NY: Sadlier, 1979), 193.

Authors

AGNES CUNNINGHAM, SSCM, theologian and patristic scholar, is professor of patrology and director of the department of church history at St. Mary of the Lake Seminary in Mundelein, Illinois. She is past president of the Catholic Theological Society of America. Among her recent publications are *The Bishop in the Church: Patristic Texts on the Role of the* Episkopos and *Prayer: Personal and Liturgical.*

CATHERINE DOOLEY, OP, is an assistant professor of catechetics and sacraments in the department of religion and religious education at the Catholic University of America in Washington DC. Her religious education writings include *The Jesus Book, The Mary Book, The Saints Book* and *The Gift of Peace.* Her liturgical writings have appeared in *New Catholic World, Catechumenate: A Journal of Christian Initiation* and *New Catholic Encyclopedia.*

JAMES B. DUNNING, priest of the archdiocese of Seattle, is president of the North American Forum on the Catechumenate. He is a speaker and author on RCIA, education, catechesis, sacramentality and theology.

RON LEWINSKI, priest of the archdiocese of Chicago, is director of the Office for Divine Worship, Chicago. He is the author of *Guide for Sponsors, Welcoming the New Catholic* and *How Does a Person Become a Catholic?* He is on the steering committee of the North American Forum on the Catechumenate.

GILBERT OSTDIEK, OFM, teaches liturgy at the Catholic Theological Union in Chicago. He holds an STD degree and is author of numerous articles on liturgy and sacramental theology. He has done extensive work with continuing adult education in the area of liturgy.

MARIE SEAMAN, SFCC, has worked in elementary education, preschool program development, school and CCD administration, and liturgical consultation. She has written various educational materials, including *Baptism Is a Beginning.* Currently she coordinates family, child and sacrament catechesis for rural parishes in the archdiocese of Louisville.

GERARD S. SLOYAN, a priest of the diocese of Trenton, is professor of religion at Temple University. He received the John Courtney Murray Award of the Catholic Theological Society in 1981. He has written many books on catechetics, scripture, worship and interfaith relations.

JAMES A. WILDE is an editor for Liturgy Training Publications in Chicago. He coauthored *When Catholics Speak about Jews* with John Pawlikowski and he edits *Catechumenate: A Journal of Christian Initiation* and the *Font and Table* series of books related to the sacraments of baptism, confirmation and eucharist.